I dedicate this book to all of the determined people
with disabilities who came before me and fought hard
for the rights I have today. Without their tireless work,
things would have been very different for me.

—**Belo Miguel Cipriani**

Contents

Introduction

Ten years ago, I found myself desperately looking for disability stories. I was twenty-seven years old, newly blind, and was eager for some form of confirmation that I was not alone. That I was not the only disabled man with the desire to get a job or date. That somewhere in the vast world, there was someone else also dealing with the constant, intimate questions from strangers: Were you born blind? Who dresses you? Have you looked into stem cell research? Why not?

As a gay teen, I found great comfort in the writings of Gore Vidal, James Baldwin, and Edmund White. So, it felt pretty natural to seek comfort in literature once I learned the rest of my life would be spent in darkness.

Every week, while struggling to use the white cane, I would slowly move through the main entrance of the San Francisco Public Library on Larkin Street. Elated, I'd step up to the reference desk to pick up a new pile of audio books. Some of the plastic CD cases were worn and smelled like vanilla and almonds. Other books were massive and needed several rubber bands to hold the thick stack of CDs together.

On my way back home from the library, I would hear the *beep! beep!* from the bus door and the chatter from the crowd around me fade, as I hit the play button on my Discman. While some stories put a smile on my face, more often than not, I found myself shaking my head with annoyance at the disabled characters in the stories I heard.

In fiction, I often found the physical limitations of a character were used as the primary source of their villainy. Men and women were painted to be pure evil as a result of a missing limb or sense. Even worse, though, was to see people, whose body showed some diversity in biology, be simply shown as charity cases.

In the world of memoir, the reading options for disability stories were limited. In fact, they were almost non-existent. Many books that were labeled as disability stories, turned out to be about people, who were told, after a tragedy, that they would never walk, see, or speak again, beat all odds and miraculously get their abilities back. Thus, the protagonist ends up not having to live with their condition—an option not available to most people with disabilities.

As I progressed in my rehabilitation, and technology improved, I ditched the bulky CD cases first for an e-reader, then a tablet, and finally for an app on my smartphone. Each piece of technology helped me to expand my search for disability stories further -- to blogs, to podcasts and to social media. Yet these stories remained difficult to find. Eventually, my constant unsuccessful searches for people like me pushed me to become a writer. Storytelling soon became my life, and writing granted me several wonderful opportunities.

Perhaps one of the most unexpected outcomes of the writing life was the opportunity to travel. I spent summers in New England at artist colonies, spoke at writing conferences in Europe, and guest lectured at universities around the globe. With my yellow, forty-five pound guide dog, Madge, and later with my second guide dog, Oslo, a seventy-five pound black lab, I would shake large and small hands at literary events, always on the lookout for other storytellers with disabilities.

I met all manner of folk at these artsy happenings, yet the majority of them were able-bodied. Still, it was at one of these colonies that I had an epiphany.

At a large barn in upstate New York, I sat on a squeaky wooden chair as a painter sketched my face. As I heard his pencil trace the paper, I vented to him about my frustration on the lack of good literary interpretations of disability in books. With a nonchalant expression in his voice, he suggested, "Maybe you should do some journalism. You can help get more stories out there."

In the humid room, I felt a cool rush of excitement coat my body. While I had not considered journalism as a career path, the idea made sense.

A few months later, I was writing for the *San Francisco Chronicle*, and contributing to several radio shows, but my biggest win was when the news editor at the *Bay Area Reporter*, accepted my pitch to have a column solely dedicated to disability news.

For the first time in my writing career, I was helping other people, who some may deem to have limiting conditions, tell their stories. Among the athletes, musicians, politicians, and various professionals with disabilities I interviewed, a common thread was that they were regularly the first to do something in their communities: first deaf person to lead a theatrical play in their high school, first quadriplegic to attend their small liberal arts college, and first person with a disability at their work site. Using my talking software for the blind to document their experiences, I would reflect on the times I had been the first blind guy to do certain things. I could not help but wonder: when will people with disabilities stop being first at anything?

The constant use of the word "first" in my headlines pushed me to think about how little discussion there is of the rites of passage of people with disabilities.

It was then and there that the idea for this book was born, and the long journey collecting these stories began. For three years, I read hundreds of stories from authors that answered my call for submissions.

I would not dare to assume what each of the eleven selected authors was going through when they wrote these essays. I can, though, say these personal stories all possessed elements of suspense, surprise, and humor, and are incredibly raw. These are the kind of stories I wish I could have read ten years ago.

As the editor of this collection, I hope these eleven authors and their stories move you as much as they moved me.

—Belo Miguel Cipriani

Life with Lexie
Heidi Johnson-Wright

At age nine, severe rheumatoid arthritis hijacked my life. The disease's rapid course over the next few years ravaged my joints, making it difficult to walk, wash my hair—even put on a shirt. I could no longer do things I'd previously done with ease. My mom became my primary caregiver.

To outsiders, she appeared the stereotypical doting parent of a disabled child, the perfect mothering figure. But behind closed doors, my mom had another side. She seemed to struggle with inner demons that could not be tamed. On a good day, she was simply irritable. On bad days, her moods fluctuated between agitation, anger and blind rage. The slightest thing could set her off: an unexpected change of plans, a minor disappointment, or an innocent comment taken the wrong way.

I always thought of my mom's right index finger as her "witch finger." The tip of it was half the size of the others and was cloven with a nasty surgical scar, the result of a childhood infection. She often shouted while thrusting her witch finger in the air, bouncing it to and fro with each syllable uttered. It seemed her way of letting others know she was the self-appointed disciplinarian of the human race —in case her steady string of pre-judgments and priggish sensibilities weren't enough. When she was aiming the witch finger at someone else, I secretly delighted in the display of indignation. When aimed at me, I felt profoundly lost and sad, like a motherless child.

For a small woman, my mother's footfalls were thundering. I could hear her walking from nearly any corner of the house. It was as if her mission in life was to stomp the devil back down to hell. She was deceptively strong. She could lift heavy objects and scoot large appliances across the floor. Many times, she cut the lawn to help out my dad, pushing the mower with a ferocity I admired. Few of the other moms in our neighborhood were willing to so boldly step out of their assigned gender roles.

My mother was a straight-laced, dry Methodist, and her laces were often stretched to the brink. She had no middle ground. It was impossible for her to utter the adjective "red" without preceding it with "fiery." Night was "*pitch* black," and winter days, "*freezing* cold." She loved things, never liked them; hated things, never simply disliked them. She pronounced experiences as "absolutely fantastic" or "terrible, horrible."

Despite her demons, there were times when she cared for me with thoughtful tenderness. Yet even on those days, I tried my best to stay on her good side. Take my word for it; you don't want to piss off the person who wipes your ass.

As a kid, I had no clue her baffling mood swings were symptomatic of a personality disorder. I didn't know that cruel mental demons sometimes made her life unbearable. I only knew I did not want to fuck with her. And the worst possible way to fuck with my mom was to upset her Queen Anne furniture, matching napkin rings, garden club flower shows, and Laura Ashley way of life.

A couple years after my diagnosis, it was clear my disease had no plans to depart. It had entrenched itself like an unwanted houseguest. Climbing the stairs up to my room became impossible. Each night, my dad had to haul me up like a sack of potatoes and back down the next morning.

Neighbors would suggest turning our family room into a bedroom, and enlarging the downstairs bath. Relatives would ask when we were moving to a single-story home. None of it amounted to anything, really. There were never any family meetings around the dinner table to discuss options.

Looking back, it seems utterly ridiculous. Why didn't our family take steps to make the house welcoming to me? Didn't my parents want to make their lives easier? Every dead lift up the stairs, every tricky transfer into the shower drained their energy and put them at risk of injury. Sometimes, with my adult sensibilities, I can make sense of portions of my childhood. On this topic, I fail utterly.

Talk did come up in passing about installing a stair climber on a track up the stairs, which could take me up and down at the touch of a button. Several times, when her friends were over and my father was not around, my mom would pointedly speak loud enough for me to overhear: "It'll look terrible. It will just ruin the look of the house. It'll be the first thing people see when they come in the door."

Overhearing this paralyzed me with dread. I would have welcomed an easy way up the stairs. But I was also horribly embarrassed that I couldn't just run up them under my own steam, the way I used to scale trees. Maybe I simply wasn't trying hard enough. And what kid wants to have to depend on a contraption normally used by old geezers? I also felt ashamed of my neediness, which was negatively impacting my parents' finances and my mom's pride in her beautiful home.

One day, when she and I were alone, my mom asked me about it out of the blue.

"What do you think we should do? Should we install a stair climber? You'll be the one using it, so you should decide."

My mom never willingly handed off the right to make important decisions to others—certainly not to me. I knew this was a calculated move on her part, and there was only one right response.

Game, set, match: Mom. No stair climber for our house.

This was the only model of the attendant/client relationship I'd ever known: a short-tempered caregiver dressing and showering me in an utterly inaccessible home.

Then college came along, and I had to hire and manage my first work-for-pay personal care attendant. I hadn't the slightest idea how to go about it. Hell, I didn't even know which college was a good match for me, given my hips, knees and ankles were more suited for a golden-ager nursing home.

***

Decades before the ADA, Kent State University nurtured a reputation as an inclusive institution. It was also known for politically minded free thinkers, and was the school where national guardsmen shot four students to death during a Vietnam War protest on May 4, 1970. By the eighties, Kent had lost much of its radical edginess and established itself as an excellent state university.

My parents were slow to accept that Kent was no longer a hub of hemp-wearing, longhaired political revolutionaries. But because of my disability, my college options were extremely limited. My only two choices were to attend some marginally accessible university—living in an off-campus apartment with my mother as roommate, caregiver, chauffeur and chastity enforcer—or to go to KSU. Given these options, I would have eagerly become a quadruple amputee had it been a pre-requisite for admission to Kent.

Most of Kent's classroom buildings were wheelchair accessible, as were the student center, library and campus bookstore. Female undergraduates with disabilities were housed on the first floor of one dorm, with the only accessible men's dorm across the street. Disabled students got to class via a door-to-door lift-van service. The university even recruited students interested in working as personal care attendants, and then held a daylong event in the summer, at which we freshman gimps could interview the pre-screened candidates.

When that day arrived, we gathered—some of us struggling to walk, others in wheelchairs—to learn how to manage an attendant. For most of us, this would be the first time we'd ever been helped with dressing, bathing or wiping our backsides by someone other than a family member.

I felt a slight thrill of liberation at the prospect, tempered with a healthy dose of trepidation. I had no problem getting naked in front of a stranger; I'd done my Gypsy Rose Lee act in front of scores of nurses and doctors in hospitals. My concern was finding someone I could depend on. How would I know which candidate could be trusted to haul her butt out of bed and get me ready on time, and which loser would hit the snooze button on her alarm five times each morning, ensuring I miss my van ride to class?

The afternoon was a blur of interviews with candidates—most Kent students themselves—who rotated around the room to be interviewed by us students. It was like speed dating for crips and caregivers, but without martinis and mood lighting. I took notes on each girl, but by late afternoon, I was growing fuzzy-brained. By day's end, I had trouble matching names with faces, but one face stood out.

Alexis had big green eyes and wild, dishwater-blonde tresses. She looked like a cross between a young Dyan Cannon and a punk rock Betty Boop. I felt an immediate connection. She was enthusiastic, but not fawning, and clearly had a sense of humor. She knew Kent well—both the university and the town—since she'd lived nearby her whole life. Like me, Alexis—or Lexie—was an English major. She promised to give me the inside scoop on the professors. She was perfect.

When I called Lexie the next day to extend an offer, she accepted. We nailed down the details for her first day of work. Everything seemed to be aligning. But when I hung up the phone, I couldn't quite shake a feeling of unease. Perhaps I was simply jittery about the big, grand adventure of college. Or perhaps it was because I'd soon be relying on a stranger: a person who could either help make my next four years a spectacular success or an abject failure.

***

When I moved into my dorm during freshman week, I was excited, but anxious. There were van rides to be scheduled, books to be bought, dorm mates to meet, and cafeteria foods to be avoided.

In between chats with girls on my floor and Lexie's twice-daily visits, I was a teary-eyed, nervous wreck. Some anxiety was because I'd been uprooted to a strange place with few familiar faces. But what really made my palms sweat was being uncertain of how much walking I would have to do each day once classes started. My parents had bought me a manual wheelchair, but I had neither the strength nor agility to push myself in it. Its only value was an occasional short trip with someone pushing me. Getting to the vans, to class, to the cafeteria—to virtually everywhere—would require a lot of walking.

Obsessive thoughts began to burst out from creaky, crooked doors inside my head that I thought had been nailed shut. What if the walking was simply too much? What if I had a flare or sudden pain that kept me off my feet? What if I missed too many classes and flunked out?

Some say the road to hell is paved with good intentions. The road to my own personal hell was a rancid, oozing quicksand of "what ifs" that was pulling me under, inch by inch. I had to find a way to break free if I was going to survive.

***

Lexie is resting her foot in my lap; I am painting her toenails. I'm using small, careful brushstrokes of a frosted pink polish. I want to do a good job. Her boyfriend, a young Tom Hanks lookalike, has requested certain preparations. He wants to suck her toes on their next date.

I have learned a great deal about Lexie in just a few short weeks, and am learning more right now as she chatters on about her family, her dating history, and her friends. She's a bit wilder than I'd originally pegged her for. She enjoys mood-altering substances, but nothing hardcore. No needle drugs. And she's had plenty of boyfriends. I have a tough time keeping track as she shares anecdotes about them: some raunchy, some sweet. Her musical tastes are eclectic, to say the least. She loves punk bands, but she's also an Elton John fanatic.

Lexie lives at home fifteen minutes from campus with her parents. Because Lexie doesn't drive (for reasons she hasn't explained), her dad chauffeurs her back and forth to campus. So far, she's been on time every day to help me get ready in the morning and to help me shower and prep for bed at night.

I'm still waking up each morning nauseous from nerves—sometimes even puking. But right at this moment—sitting in my standard, university-issue desk chair, in this institutional, mid-century dorm room, with its green linoleum and god-awful drapes—I feel happy, even a little euphoric. When I tell Lexie a joke that pokes fun at disabled people, but is straight-up hilarious, she laughs—shakes even—from her head down to her pink-lacquered toes. Other people I've told that joke to freeze just after I deliver the punch line, afraid to laugh. Lexie shows no such fear.

She has passed my little test.

***

I could major in anything and still be considered pre-law. I chose English because I loved to read, loved language and aspired to be a writer. Emphasis on "aspired."

One evening, I sat in my room, searching for fodder for a poem I was certain was inside me. I felt blank. I felt like a fraud. I wasn't the least bit excited at the prospect of going to law school in a few years. Nor was I the creative writer I longed to be.

I'd met young people my age that could write as naturally as they breathed. Lexie was one of them. So were many of her friends. Lexie had introduced me to her artsy pals who gathered in the Student Center cafeteria or the English building. I loved her introductions because they diverged so far from my mom's *Leave It to Beaver* standards of good taste: "This is Heidi. You'll notice she's very short. So short that guys ask her to 'go up' on them."

Lexie's friends were pleasant and polite, but I felt like they could see right through me, that they were probably thinking, *little girl from the 'burbs, dabbler, poseur.*

I wasn't sure that I really fit in. They were serious about their art, and had plans to get their MFAs and write novels, or get their band's demo into the hands of a Geffen Records' exec, or move to New York to apprentice as a jewelry designer. I knew I didn't belong with the campus Republicans for Reagan. But just because I lived in the gimp ghetto didn't necessarily mean I fit in perfectly with all the other gimps.

I was dependent on my parents and I didn't know how to break free. Just thinking about it made me feel like a whiny, pathetic little bitch. The more self-loathing I churned up, the more powerless I felt.

***

For my first creative writing class, I kept a journal in which I recorded flitting thoughts and germinating ideas that sometimes became lines of poetry. Rarely was it good poetry, but the fact that I had enough self-confidence to put it on paper was, for me, a courageous act.

I took inspiration wherever I could find it. From music and movies and the writing of others. From student art shows and dance recitals. From the ebb and flow of gimp dorm life.

And I looked to Lexie as my Svengali and role model. I wanted to write like her, spew snark like her and, of course, dress like her. With an eye for thrift store treasures, Lexie might pair a man's green sport jacket with a black mini skirt and textured stockings. She could also work a more androgynous look of a boy's ochre cable knit sweater and a pair of seventies, brown, striped trousers.

After a few fashion faux pas, I finally learned to dress the part of an eighties liberal arts sprite. Black, straight-leg jeans were a must. The slightest flare of the pant leg put you back in high school with the stoners who wore suede fringed moccasin boots. No designer name on the ass: no exceptions.

Lexie sometimes wore vintage bowling shirts with men's names in cursive on the chest—like Buddy or Mel or Mac. I raided my grandfather's closet and hit pay dirt: a sixties Black Label Beer bowling shirt. I nicked a half dozen of my dad's old ties he hadn't worn since LBJ was in office, and altered them until they were crazy-narrow. I couldn't tie a Windsor knot to save my life, but Lexie could.

The bigger the hair, the better. I didn't have the nerve to bleach my locks and tease them like an MTV video vixen. But I kept the curly perm that made my head look like a topiary sculpture. Lexie sculpted it each day with a plastic pick.

My ears weren't pierced, so I became a connoisseur of clip-on earrings from thrift stores and flea markets. Large geometric shapes with bold colors went nicely with big hair. Matching pairs were too "sorority girl," so I wore three different earrings at the same time: sometimes a gold dangly and pink seashell on one ear, a black heart on the other.

My wardrobe's *piece de resistance* was a pair of black, faux-leather slacks. Because they had a vinyl texture, I had to be careful how I moved in them. If I scooted too hard across a chair, they made an embarrassing farting sound. And I didn't care they made my ass look like the seat of a Barcalounger. Simply putting them on my made me feel cooler.

I was so ready for 1983.

***

College expanded my horizons beyond *Beowulf* and Byzantine art and the Great Chain of Being. I began to see that living in a place without steps and with roll-in showers made life a hell of a lot easier. Being able to go to my room whenever I wanted or to bathe without drama was amazing. I didn't have to ask someone to drag me up a flight of steps, risking their back and my ribs.

It was also a revelation to have a caregiver who wasn't my mom. Lexie showed up twice a day because it was her job. She wasn't a family member obligated to help and resentful because of it. When she put on my socks or washed my hair, she didn't drop emotional blackmail shit-bombs in my lap. Instead, she told me about Mick Jagger eating an acid-laced Milky Way out of Marianne Faithfull's girlie parts, or how she felt the first time she read *Naked Lunch*.

I saw Lexie as both caregiver and nurturing older sister. With the steady strength of her small hands, often chilled by Ohio's cold weather, she made me feel safe. She helped me with dressing, grooming—even cleaning up the morning after a night of heavy menstrual flow. She toasted my morning pop tarts and heated Jeno's Pizza Rolls just right. She brought me tea and Jell-O when I had a ferocious stomach flu, cleaned out my barf bucket and laundered the undies I'd shat in. She never made me feel guilty for needing help and often found humor in it.

She shared her jewelry collection with me and told me which tops flattered my tits. She decorated my room, taping up my Thomas Dolby poster and sundry photos torn from *Spin* and *Melody Maker*. She brought me her brother's back issues of *Creem*, because she knew I'd dig Lester Bangs. She gave me her sister's vintage dresses and cargo jeans, which fit me perfectly. She bought me Lou Reed's *Growing Up in Public* album, which she'd found in a discount store cut-out bin. I played the shit out of that damn record, because I dug Lou Reed, but mostly because it came from her.

Sometimes—okay, often—we talked about sex. I had no experience on that account, but enjoyed Lexie's anecdotes about birth control and pregnancy scares and the simple joy of the act. I lived vicariously through her, but part of me felt like a worthless schlub. She was Kiki de Montparnasse and I was Laura Wingfield from *The Glass Menagerie.*

I trusted Lexie with my very well being, because we'd forged an emotional bond. When your surrogate sister speaks candidly about masturbation and orgasms and locating her cervix, about creepy relatives and sad, messy breakups with boyfriends, it means something.

As our relationship deepened, an implicit, unspoken agreement arose. She would nurture and care for me, but we were never to discuss it. She might express affection through gifts of earrings or meticulously ironing one of my blouses. Deeds, never words. Anytime our conversations ever danced along the edge of sentimentality, she would immediately pull back, sometimes even hurling an insult. She might say an outfit made me look like a pathetic virgin, or that I would never break free of my sanitized suburban upbringing. The jabs would re-establish just enough space, saving us both from the clutches of emotional vulnerability.

Lexie was the punk poetess I wanted to be. She never went anywhere without a black, fine-tip, felt pen and a crazy sheaf of papers sticking out of her purse, jotting down ideas and couplets and sometimes whole poems in a matter of minutes. She was a fearsome female force whose provocative verse burst forth from her pen like lightening from the clouds. She wrote with the effortlessness of breathing, unafraid to explore whatever direction it might take her.

I think she knew I'd never write anything worthwhile until I broke out of the prison of my middle-class mindset. I'd been raised to follow rules unquestioningly, to not simply obey authority, but to venerate it. Like an uptight little ninny, I was petrified of even getting a blue slip, a demerit for low-level infractions of dorm conduct code, like cranking up the stereo too loud or entertaining a visitor past curfew. I was sure I was just one slip-up away from a slippery slope of getting kicked out of school.

Sometimes, Lexie made jabs at my "rules weenie" mentality, which I took in stride. Occasionally, she could be shrill, even mean-spirited. If I saw her face twist into a certain disgusted smirk, I felt my heart sink. It meant my coolness quotient had taken a dive.

One morning, as she was leaving my room, John Cougar Mellencamp's "The Authority Song" came on the radio. As she walked away, I could hear her voice in the corridor, parodying the lyrics: "Heidi loves authority, and she always will/she never fights authority, authority always wins."

***

At the start of sophomore year, I returned to school still struggling with anxiety, but some of my fears had burned away. I'd mastered the van system, and how to manage my rides to class. I had my own private sanctuary: a dorm room intended for two students, but only housing one. My parents felt I needed the space for my newly acquired power wheelchair, which I could drive on my own. The added privacy was nice, given all of the sex I wasn't having.

My first week back, it was great to see Lexie's Kohl-lined blue eyes again, to smell her fragrance of soft perfume mixed with cigarette smoke. She was full of stories about how she'd spent the summer, the bands she'd gone to see and the writing she'd done. She could go to 7-Eleven for a candy bar and come away with a hilarious, twenty-minute anecdote to tell, full of intricate detail.

What concerned me, though, was her growing attachment to a girl named Audrey. I knew girls like Audrey, even had cousins like her. Girls who took their scores on *Cosmo* magazine quizzes very seriously. Hillbilly flibbertigibbets that had nothing going for them—no brains, or money, or legitimate ambition. Their stock-in-trade was manipulation. They cut themselves, or faked pregnancies, or claimed to have exotic diseases, so others would rush to their side and rescue them.

Over the summer, Audrey had moved in with Lexie and chauffeured her to and from campus. Now their relationship gave off an unhealthy vibe, as if Lexie had allowed herself to become too dependent, too wrapped up in Audrey's personal drama. Their friendly symbiosis felt more like parasitic predation.

Thrown into this mix was Elliot, a guy who Lexie had a crush on. His aloofness never allowed me to get a true read on him. At first, I assumed he avoided eye contact simply because he was shy. But when he smugly dismissed my U.S. release version of Thomas Dolby's *The Golden Age of Wireless*, because its song mixes differed from the U.K. release, I wanted to smack the smirk off his face. He seemed a privileged preppie that looked down his nose at anyone who hadn't backpacked through Europe the summer after high school. To Lexie, he was a gifted writer and poet, a young Rimbaud who would take her on a leopard skin rug by firelight. I wasn't so sure he was right for Lexie, but I was a naïve, little, virgin nobody from suburbia. What the hell did I know?

***

And so, the four of us—Lexie, Audrey, Elliot and me—find ourselves in my dorm room on a glorious Northeastern Ohio September evening, the sun's last rays turning the sky turquoise and fuchsia and periwinkle.

We're just hanging out, and I harbor no illusions that I'm actually part of this dynamic. I'm merely providing the space for this collegiate literary salon/pheromone exchange, much like the front desk guy at a pay-by-the-hour motel.

I'm getting schooled on the subtleties of English lit eye fucking, as Lexie and Elliot trade glances and flirtatious remarks, thinly veiled as pithy poetic lines. Audrey can't keep up, obtuse to references to Yeats and Pound, Kerouac and Ginsberg. All she has to contribute are her hillbilly-pretty cheekbones, and her cosmetology skills, as she applies eye shadow to Elliot's lids.

Spandau Ballet's "True" comes on the radio and Audrey—who must always be the center of attention—stands transfixed for a moment. She begins to sway back and forth, a trailer-trash train wreck.

Audrey's eyes are closed as she lip-syncs the lead vocals. I spend this awkward moment reading facial expressions. Elliot wishes Audrey was studying for her GED in a double-wide far, far away. Lexie realizes her girlfriend doesn't know a Norton anthology from a Chia Pet. But Audrey's all-American Ralph Lauren model looks always turn heads. And Lexie sadly lacks confidence in her own short, curvy, punk girl beauty. She feels compelled to drag Audrey along wherever she goes, like some sort of low rent femme fatale from a Tennessee Williams play, a boy-magnet good luck charm in cha-cha heels.

Lexie has become far more to me than simply a caregiver. I worry about her, knowing that self-doubt can lead to bad choices in friends.

***

At Halloween, I had no boyfriend and no parties to go to. But college had taught me how to enjoy time alone. My room was no Parisian garret apartment, but it was my very own space. I didn't have to explain to anyone why I wanted to tape a photo on the wall of Lou Reed and David Bowie kissing, or why I wrote lines of militant feminist poetry in red ink on a maxi pad and stuck it to the mirror. I didn't have to worry about my mom's unannounced prison cell-style searches. I did not miss her tossing my belongings as she pleased, histrionically gasping and exclaiming, "What *is* this?" Then, feasting on the terrified look on my face.

Lexie had big plans for Halloween and I was getting a thrill of vicarious enjoyment as she shared the details. For several weeks, she'd been assembling the perfect costume: a vintage lace-up corset, dyed black, a black mini skirt, and fishnet stockings. The outfit transformed her into the Julie Newmar version of Cat Woman with a dash of Morticia Addams.

Elliot was going as Hamlet, complete with doublet, stockings, and skull. The two of them were still engaged in a dance consisting of poetry workshopping one moment and sexually charged verbal *pas de deux* the next. Their Halloween plans were to drop acid, then hit the bars downtown. Elliot's dorm room would be the end-of-the-night crash pad. I had no idea what his intentions were, but it was clear Lexie wanted to take their flirty friendship to the next level. Complicating everything was the fact that Audrey would be tagging along.

When the big night arrived, Lexie came to my room early to prep and primp. She was ebullient, talking rapid fire. I was happy for her, but a little sad, too. There were only so many years of college with holidays that were a perfect excuse for dressing up slutty and imbibing to excess. Was I missing out?

Maybe I should have dressed up as a French maid and thrown myself at one of the guys in the male gimp ghetto across the street. But the boys with cerebral palsy scared me a little. What would happen if a guy with a spastic jaw went down on me? There were a couple of cute paraplegic boys. Problem was, I didn't know what to do exactly with a boner, let alone one that was catheterized.

Love could be so fucking complicated.

***

I wake up to Rick Springfield singing "Affair of the Heart." It's bad enough the girls in the room next door to me love the boyish Australian singing sensation and probably rub one out now and then as they gaze at his poster on their wall. That they are blasting his bubblegum garbage this early in the morning makes me want to bitch slap them both.

I can already tell it will be an overcast, gray-sky day. I turn on my stereo, hoping some good tunes will help me shake loose the mental cobwebs. I am still thinking this is just a day like any other when I suddenly remember Lexie's big night. I look at the clock radio and realize she will arrive any minute now.

Soon I hear Lexie approaching from halfway down the hall. She has a certain gait, a way she carries herself in her Keds—her walking shoes—along with her purse and ever-present, huge tote bag. She makes a characteristic *stomp-swish-stomp-swish* sound that I can identify with ease.

I figure after being out all night, she will look worse for wear. Still, I am not quite prepared for what I see when the door swings open.

Lexie's hair is a matted mess, her makeup grotesquely smeared like wet road kill. She is clad partly in her costume and partly in street clothes, like a witch who ducked out of a black mass, threw on jeans and ran out for a pack of cigarettes. The moment she closes the door, she slumps down to the floor and groans. Not the kind of groans you make when you've partied all night and your engine is finally winding down. Instead, they are the groans that come from sorrow and shattered expectations.

That's when I realize Lexie's eyes are red and puffy— not from caked mascara, but from sobbing. My stomach clenches like a fist. I've known Lexie for over a year, during which she's had several breakups with boyfriends and other personal drama. I have never seen her in tears, have never imagined my punk poetess/caregiver, with the flinty charm and emotional armor, could even cry.

For the next half hour, words and more tears flow forth as I listen. Her narrative is convoluted, turns back on itself at times. I have so many questions, but I don't dare interrupt. For the first time in our employment arrangement turned friendship, I sense that Lexie needs me as much as I need her.

Lexie's evening began when she, Elliot and Audrey each dropped acid. Soon it became obvious something was horribly wrong. They felt as if their hearts were battering their chests from the inside, trying to leap out. Then came shakiness and nausea. Lexie tried to push through her own pain and drug-induced paranoia. Could they walk off the symptoms and press on? Or should they head to a hospital ER?

Lexie begins to sob now. She recalls sitting down on the sidewalk while diapered frat boys dressed as giant babies and girls costumed as sexy kittens passed by carrying red Solo cups.

Her narrative breaks down now and I am unclear about what happens next. All I know is that Hamlet, the sensuous Wiccan and the hillbilly train wreck end up back in Elliot's dorm room. Lexie was distraught, profoundly disappointed that her big Halloween had become a giant fiasco. She was also worried about her own health. Could any of those seventies rumors of LSD cut with strychnine be true?

This is when her closest gal pal and her potential new boyfriend should have seen Lexie's pain and rallied around her. Instead, they began a make-out session for Lexie's viewing pleasure.

I am stunned. In the previous twelve hours, Lexie has been betrayed by her best friend, taken ill herself and—perhaps worst of all—come to the realization that perhaps she and Elliot were not meant to be lovers.

She is lying in a heap on my floor, in need of comforting that I don't know how to give. Coming from a WASP-y, pull up your socks and trudge on kind of family, comforting was a skill that did not come naturally. She is Sally Bowles and I am Heidi of the Swiss Alps. What could I possibly do to help her?

A few days later, Lexie is stricken with a severe flu and a bout of laryngitis. She is much too sick to work, so I temporarily hire an attendant already employed by another girl down the hall. My sub is pleasant and punctual, but resembles Dick Butkus in bibbed overalls. She's never heard of Captain Sensible or seen *I Am Curious (Yellow)*, nor does she have an opinion as to what is the most genteel, literary word for "vagina." (Lexie and I have agreed on "quim.") I soon develop an irrational dislike for the poor woman, though I try not to show it. I deeply miss Lexie and fret about her health.

Finally, after two weeks, my door swings open one morning. "I had a dream last night I was serving spaghetti to Chico Marx and he had a huge fucking boner!"

Thank God Lexie was back.

***

My baby steps in becoming a writer included taking my first poetry workshop class. Up to that point, I had written mostly prose, but I now saw the world differently. I had begun to feel the magic in language. I found myself observing how sounds fit together or jangled against each other. How the most mundane words could sometimes hold profound meaning.

But what if I truly had nothing to say or my stuff was pitifully derivative? Upping the ante was the fact that Lexie and staff from the *New Kent Quarterly*, an English department poetry publication, would be my classmates. One moment I felt enthralled by it all; the next, I cursed myself for being a total out-of-my-depth dumbass.

I sought writing inspiration everywhere. When something caught my attention—even two or three words—I jotted it down on my cardboard desk blotter, between ads by local businesses and Kent State's football schedule. If Lexie uttered a funny line or wacky observation ("jizz is just virulent snot"), it made the blotter. If I became enchanted with a lyric from a Lou Reed song ("quasi-effeminate characters in love with oral gratification"), it made the blotter. If I was fortunate enough to come up with a line or two of my own (I once wrote an assonance-filled and decidedly unreadable poem about Zoroastrianism), it found its place on the blotter, perhaps bookended by a pizza grease spot and an ad for the university bookstore.

A sluice gate had been opened in my mind. I prayed what poured out wasn't simply a river of shit.

***

Dr. L was our poetry workshop professor. He had white hair, soft blue eyes, and a gentle demeanor. He was the type of person I could never imagine angry. He began the semester teaching basics about feet and meter. I dutifully copied down the definitions of "spondee" and "trochee," "iambic" and "anapestic." After the first couple of classes, we were expected to write poems and submit them each week for review by our classmates.

Besides me, there was Lexie, who could write poetry because she thought, talked, perhaps even fucked in poetry (or at least fucked a couple of other poets). Put a black, fine-tip felt pen in her hand and she'd soon be writing deep shit on sheets of paper, desktops—maybe even tampon wrappers.

Gay Sonnet Writer was the type of guy that Lexie referred to as "professionally gay," like the guys who wear T-shirts that say, "I'm so gay I shit rainbows." He was very sweet and kind when commenting on the poetry of others.

Bulimia Girl got her nickname because she wrote a poem that repeated the line "you leave me" over and over, until it sounded like the word "bulimia." Lexie and I speculated she was a closeted, self-hating lesbian. That theory became fact in our minds when we heard Bulimia Girl had accosted Gay Sonnet Writer in the Student Center and declared she didn't approve of his lifestyle. I henceforth dismissed her as a sanctimonious, little god twaddler.

Pendulous Breasts wrote mostly what Lexie called "bad boyfriend poetry." Sometimes the adjective "bad" modified the word "boyfriend" and other times it modified the word "poetry." Now and then, it modified both. Pendulous Breasts once submitted a poem for workshopping, but said it was too emotional for her to read aloud in class. Everyone looked at each other awkwardly until Dr. L read it aloud for her. The level of discomfort in the classroom rose appreciably when he got to a graphic part about a big, sloppy blowjob.

Lazy Eye Girl was an odd duck. Her oddness had nothing to do with her amblyopia, but rather her general demeanor and stilted way of speaking. Unlike the rest of us, she was obsessed with traditional forms of rhyme and meter. She struck me as a Ren-fest chronic, although I had no evidence to support this. Her opinions about my work were often cryptic, though never unkind.

Skinny Van Driver Chick worked for the campus bus service driving gimps like me to class. She conjured powerful images with just a few lines, never using one word more than needed.

Hipster in the Greek Fisherman's Hat rolled his own cigarettes and sported a goatee years before they came back into style. He could write poetry reminiscent of a Tom Waits song, something that made you want to laugh, cry, and hide under the bed—all at the same time.

Crazy in Love Couple were gifted writers, but their talents were in cold storage. Every ounce of their energy was spent mooning over each other. This was reflected in their tepid poetry, but no one wanted to point this out. They were just so damn cute together.

By semester's end, I gained some much-needed confidence about my work. I would never be Stevie Smith, but that was okay. Sometimes, knowing your limits is just as liberating as owning your strengths.

***

Eddie sat a couple rows behind me in Psych of Adjustment class. I barely noticed him the first few weeks of the semester. But Eddie noticed me. One day, he came over to ask me a question about Albert Ellis and rational emotive therapy. Tall, gawky and bespectacled, with a wild shock of red hair, he looked like a Muppet that had broken free of his handler. I wasn't sure what to make of him. He seemed gentle and unassuming, and I pegged him as one of those nerdy boys who was taught to be kind to babies, kittens, and gimp girls.

Soon we were chatting before and after class, and our conversations began to transcend schoolwork. I soon realized Eddie's knowledge about movies was encyclopedic. He could rattle off in under a minute the title of every film that had ever won the Oscar for best picture.

Eddie and I spent the better part of one weekend together prepping for a mid-term. Our friendship then spilled outside the confines of psych class, and we began attending cult/art films together at a campus theater. Simply as friends, of course.

***

One balmy, breezy spring evening, Eddie invites me to come over for a game of Trivial Pursuit. I meet him at his friend's apartment. His friend is renown in Eddie's social circle as being able—with drum machine-like accuracy—to fart the opening rhythmic beats of David Bowie's "Modern Love."

I am wearing a leopard print blouse and my black pleather slacks. My mom would definitely not approve, which delights me. Lexie, on the other hand, told me proudly that I look like a video vixen. When she dressed me, however, she implored:

"Heidi, do not have sex tonight. Please—no sex yet. You've only just met this guy."

That is the Lexie I love: equal parts punk liberator and nurturing protector.

When I arrive at Eddie's friend's apartment, it seems to be on fire. Then I catch a whiff of skunky funk, and I realize it's pot smoke. XTC's "Senses Working Overtime" blasts from the stereo. On the wall, someone has painted a huge reproduction of Brian Eno's portrait from the cover of his album, *Before and After Science.*

For a couple hours, we talk, joke and laugh. Eddie predictably nails every movie question. But as the evening wears on, the game becomes incidental. We are really here to celebrate the brief, fleeting window before grad school and jobs and the tightening of life's golden handcuffs.

I glance at the clock and realize it's nearly midnight. I thank Eddie for a nice time and return to my dorm soon after. As I crawl into bed, I have a mind-blowing epiphany: I am smitten with Eddie. It feels spectacular! But will Lexie approve?

***

That summer, my life seemed a movie: a romantic comedy scored with the passionate soundtrack of Prince's "Purple Rain." Each time "When Doves Cry" came on the radio, I gyrated my gimp butt around the house, singing the lyrics: "Dig if you will the picture/of you and I engaged in a kiss/the sweat of your body covers me/Can you my darling/Can you picture this?"

Each week's routine builds up to my much-anticipated date with Eddie: Sunday service at our utterly inaccessible church, with its supremely uncomfortable wooden pews;

four days of accounting class at a local community college; one day of homework and household chores to appease my mom; and then Saturday night with Eddie.

Eddie's summer job was being an amusement park mascot, sweating under a heavy costume and taking shit from rowdy kids. On date night, he showered, changed then made the eighty-mile round trip to my house, usually arriving around 10 p.m. We'd spend the evening critiquing that summer's videos in MTV heavy rotation.

When I was sure my parents were asleep, we had prolonged make-out sessions on the couch. Eddie's kisses could be sweet and soft and, other times, passionate and deep. We'd embrace and melt into each other in a scent cloud of Brut, female moisture and sweat. The intensity of it all was captivating and, sometimes, a bit scary.

Sometimes just before he left, Eddie would softly sing thirties and forties standards to me, with their images of romantic starry skies: "Polka Dots and Moonbeams," "It's Only a Paper Moon," "Stardust." Miraculously, my parents let him stay until 2 a.m. or 3 a.m., provided I unflaggingly rose for church the next morning.

In between his visits, my mind obsessed on two things: Eddie and music. I imagined myself with Cyndi Lauper in the Airstream trailer in her "Time After Time" video. I cut my hair short to look like Annie Lennox. I decided that The Cars' song "Magic" was the greatest summer anthem of all time.

My previous summer—without a boyfriend—had dragged on, but this one ended much too soon. It was back to classes and cafeteria food and dorm curfews. Best of all, back to Lexie. Our reunion was delightful. It was as if we'd been apart just three hours instead of three months.

Now that I had a serious boyfriend, how would that affect what Lexie and I shared? My caregiver and dear friend could be a whirlwind of contradictions. She believed sex was a joy, but lamented how it complicated everything. She wanted me to have a beau, but she could be overly protective. She warned me about pregnancy, but sometimes cruelly mocked me for still being a virgin. She had dated a few boys who treated her like shit, yet she sometimes made fun of Eddie: my kind, gentle boyfriend, who sang to me and didn't pressure me for sex.

Then it dawned on me: human relationships are unavoidably messy. When someone washes your hair and lets you read her poetry about losing her virginity, it creates an intimate bond that can't be easily defined.

Is it one of caregiver and client? An exchange of money for services? Friendship? Something more? Something utterly indefinable?

***

Lexie remained my caregiver, friend, protector, liberator, writing coach, role model and girl crush until I graduated. I went on to law school and a public service career. She went on to an MFA and a remarkable arc as a professor and successful, celebrated writer. We both married men who'd been dormmates at Kent.

I've since worked with scores of caregivers over the years. Some have been truly wonderful, others not so much. No one rivals Lexie. She set the bar high.

And I still agree with her that "quim" is the ideal word for girlie parts.

Dark Clouds

Nigel David Kelly

I have always tried to live my life by the old Greek saying: a healthy mind in a healthy body.

Until my mid-forties, I seemed to be succeeding in this. But it was when I reached this stage of my life that an initially small, dark cloud started to appear on my horizon. It took the form of increasing hearing loss in my right ear, along with tinnitus. Now for those of you unfamiliar with what that is, it is a noise in your ear that never goes away. It can be any sound—most often it is a ringing or buzzing noise. In my case, I can only describe it as I did so often to my wife and to my doctor: it felt like I had a hole in my ear and someone was blowing cold air into it. So I had the physical sensation of having a hole in my ear and the cold, plus the noise of blowing wind.

As you can imagine, this is very distracting and affects your ability to do even an ordinary, everyday thing like watch TV. And it makes it difficult to get to sleep. However, as years passed, I started to get used to it, and was able to reach the point where I could live with it.

Of course, I had mentioned this to my doctor, but he said I was just getting older and hearing loss was normal and to be expected. But in my mid-forties, I did not think I was old, and I certainly didn't feel old.

In fact, physically, I was in great shape. I have always been into physical fitness and sports. When I was young(er), I was into martial arts and bodybuilding. By the time I had reached my mid-forties, I had gotten into powerlifting. I had always enjoyed exercising and weight training and I would work out intensely. My wife told me she couldn't watch me train as it frightened her. So I was always very physically driven and it meant a lot to me. It was just part of my DNA.

Even as a small boy, I would go around lifting things like stones and gas cylinders. I had no idea what I was doing. I just did it. When I was nine years old, I could lift a thirty-three-pound cylinder above my head with one hand. So I was naturally strong. I was also big for my age. By the time I entered high school, I was five feet, eight inches tall. However, what I did not realize then was that while I was one of the biggest boys in my year, and as tall as, or taller than, many of the male teachers, I would not actually grow any taller. In my late teens, when I got into bodybuilding, I read an article that said research showed men who reached their full adult height early, were generally very strong. So, that was the case with me.

I remember arm wrestling a teacher at my school when I was twelve. He was in the army part time and regarded himself as strong and fit, and justifiably so. He had to declare it a draw.

I couldn't wait for my next workout to see what I could do. Add another rep; add another pound to the bar. If I couldn't train for even a few days, I would become restless, even anxious.

I put equal time and energy into my mind. I had studied most of my life; I enjoyed it and would often be doing three or even four courses at the same time. By my mid-forties, I was an honors graduate, a published author and member of Mensa. Mensa is a high IQ society. You have to sit for an intellectual evaluation exam and achieve an IQ (intelligence quota) within the top two percent of the population. I discovered I have a genius-level IQ.

I married my amazing wife Karen in 1994. Her family ancestry is French. The French family name was Curlett. Hence, her full name: Karen Curlett Kelly. But although this is generations in the past, she is very French in appearance, attitudes, and likes. Being French is just in her genes. My wife has an extraordinary strength of character and heart, with a very defined sense of right and wrong, and of how people should be treated. She is an incredibly loving, empathetic and supportive person. She is petite—five feet tall and one hundred pounds. Being small, people think they can control and bully her, until they go too far, and then—as one former work colleague stated—he thought he had lost an arm!

We live in Ireland in a beautiful, little seaside town called Newcastle, which is nestled at the foot of the famous Mourne Mountains. Our front windows look out at Slieve Donard, the highest peak. We both say that we bought our house for the view.

We haven't had children, but we are very happy. We have had to fight to overcome a number of unpleasant (some very unpleasant) things in our lives. But that has made us stronger as a couple, and has made us appreciate what we have in each other, and in our lives, more.

***

By this point in our lives, the late noughties (2005-2010), we were in a really great place. However, as the noughties passed and we got into the twenty-tens, that dark cloud was slowly getting bigger. My hearing was getting worse and so was the tinnitus. Eventually, in early 2013, my doctor agreed to send me for some tests.

Now at this time, I still didn't think this was anything serious. When I went for the first test, they couldn't find anything, and said they would have to send me for more. Maybe there just wasn't anything wrong except old age? Over the coming months, I was sent for more tests. None of these showed anything. With each test, I was becoming more convinced that nothing was wrong. My doctor was right—I was just getting older. I now was wondering if they were just going to tell me to go home. But after one of these tests still showed nothing, the doctor said he would send for an MRI scan.

MRI is short for Magnetic Resonance Imaging. You lie on a bed and they strap a mask over your face so you can't move, like Hannibal Lecter. You are then pushed into a small round chamber that is so small that my wide shoulders rubbed off the sides. You are given a "panic" button to press if it all gets too much for you. I suppose it is a bit like being put into a coffin! If you were even slightly claustrophobic, you couldn't do this. You are in this for about twenty minutes while it whirs and hums as it passes up and down your head. I know it's not supposed to be physical, but I swore I could feel it going through me.

By now it was mid-2013. It was a couple of weeks before I got a letter that the doctor wanted to see me. I still was not expecting anything really bad.

In September, when I entered the doctor's office and sat down, he talked to me casually for a few minutes before getting around to the MRI scan results. Looking back, I realize he was trying to get me relaxed. Then, he hit me with it. I will always remember the exact words he used: "We found something." Now let me give you a tip. When your doctor says to you, "We found something," it is never going to be something good.

That something was a growth in my head! The dark cloud had just become a lot bigger and moved a lot closer.

Over the next half hour he filled me in on my tumor. Firstly, he emphasized it was benign, that it was non-cancerous. It is a rare tumor, slow growing, and often it never causes any serious problems. He said the tumor was still small, that sometimes they can even stop growing, and even if it did continue to grow, it would be at least five years before it started causing me any real trouble. He told me they would monitor it with more MRI scans every six months.

Having given me these seemingly reassuring facts, he suggested I go home and look up my life insurance, because if I had critical illness coverage, I could claim on it. He had other patients with this type of tumor and they had been able to claim on their life insurance. He would fill in the necessary forms for me. Apart from that, his advice was for me to get on with my life as normal.

Well, when I got home and checked my insurance, of course I didn't have critical coverage. Over twenty years earlier, when my wife and I had taken out the insurance, we were still "young." We couldn't afford both, so we had taken out only unemployment coverage, and only for her, as I seemed to have a pretty secure job. We have never claimed on the unemployment coverage! I hope you appreciate the irony of that.

Karen was very upset, as you can imagine. But I just kept saying it could have been much worse. It could have been cancerous, and I could have had only six months to live.

So I did just as the doctor ordered. I had six monthly MRI scans, which, while showing that the tumor was growing slowly, still seemed to indicate no great cause for alarm. My hearing was continuing to deteriorate, but otherwise nothing else seemed to be wrong with me.

Now entering my fifties, I felt fine—if I ignored the deafness and tinnitus. In fact, all those tests they put me through showed all my organs are in tip top shape, I have no other physical problems, and I am as healthy as a horse. There is now a calculation that my doctor can do to assess your likelihood of having a heart attack in the next ten years. This is based on your previous lifestyle (I have never smoked and rarely drink—just the odd glass of wine with a meal), your current state of health, your fitness levels, your family medical history, etc. The average risk of heart attack for even a healthy man of my age is ten to twenty percent. Mine is two point seven percent! So that was nice to know.

During the next two years, I even became a national powerlifting champion and record holder. I became more active in the sport, helping the national organization with promoting and organizing competitions. The only concession I had to make was, during powerlifting competitions, I had to get the judge to stand close to me so I could hear his commands.

So it looked like the doctor was right. Until, that is, one day in August 2015.

***

I was sitting with Karen on our sofa watching television when I started to feel really warm. I have since described it as feeling like someone had poured a kettle of boiling water over me. The perspiration was literally dripping off me. The room started to sway and I realized I was having some form of attack. I tried not to move, as even the smallest movement made me feel sick. After a couple of minutes trying this, I realized I was going to be sick no matter what I did. I got up off the sofa and made a mad dash for the door. Fortunately, we have a downstairs toilet, which is literally just opposite the lounge door, so I ran for it and collapsed over the toilet. I spent the next two-plus hours being continuously violently sick. At the time, I didn't know how long I had been there. I lost all awareness of time. When I eventually stopped being sick, I crawled on my hands and knees upstairs, where I collapsed on the bed and lay as for dead. I must have looked frightful to my wife.

It took several days in bed to get over this. Over the next few months, I had numerous attacks like this, more than I could count. Sometimes I would have more than one in a single day. I would even wake in the night, because I was having one in my sleep. During these months, I was unable to work, but, fortunately, my employer paid sick leave.

I discovered these attacks had been caused by the tumor, which was now growing fast, and was putting pressure on my brain.

The dark cloud was now huge, and was right over me!

During the months off work, my condition followed a pattern. I would have a major attack, which would involve the usual hours of being sick, followed by days in bed. Then, over the next few weeks, I would have many more, each one a little less severe, until they would stop for short while. Then, after a few days, or a week at most, another major attack would happen and the cycle would start again.

Eventually, they would settle down to the point where I could go back to work. But the stress of trying to travel to work, and to make it through the day, would soon bring on another major attack, and so it went.

During this period, it also became clear I was no longer safe to drive. I had to declare my condition to the local driving body and so I lost my license. I have not driven since, and probably never will again.

In November 2015, I had an appointment with my doctor. She noticed my hearing was deteriorating further and decided to de-wax my ear to see if it would improve it. Immediately afterwards, it did. So that seemed to be good. However, by the time I got back home, I noticed the tinnitus was now much worse!

By the next day, I realized just how much worse. The best way I can grade it, is to say what I told my wife. If what I had been experiencing before was a ten, what I was experiencing at this point was a forty! Worse still, the sound had changed. With tinnitus, after a while, you can become habituated to it. What this means is you start to just accept it as part of your sound world and it doesn't cause the stress it used to. But this depends on the noise remaining consistent for a long time. Well, at that point, my sound had remained consistent for several years. It's like if you live near a garage. Initially, you are very aware of the noise of the engines. But after a time, if you're lucky, you start to not notice them so much. Your brain has started to accept the noises as being a part of your normal sound world.

My sound now had gotten much louder, and it had changed from the "hole in ear with cold wind" to a modulating, high-pitched buzzing sound, which went up and down. This is the worst kind of tinnitus, because the fluctuations mean it is very difficult for you to habituate to it.

This was like being tortured twenty-four hours a day. The only way I could get any relief was to play white noise in my ear. I tried so many different techniques. I bought three MP4 players and would keep two charging while I used the third. I couldn't bear to be without them. My home, which had been my sanctuary, was now a torture chamber.

By the beginning of 2016, I was also developing a hypersensitive eardrum. Looking back, I realize this was brought on by the constant white noise. But I couldn't live without it. This got so bad that I couldn't bear any noise. I would stand in front of our microwave so I could stop it a second before it finished, as the *bing!* sound it made was painful to my ear. I couldn't go to the cinema to watch a film, or to a restaurant, as most play loud music. My wife had to keep the speed in the car down to forty miles an hour, because above that, the air pressure hurt my ear.

I was still trying to get back to work and would make it in for a few days for a couple of weeks. When I got home, I would eat my dinner as quickly as I could, and then go to bed. I would try to force myself to sleep, with the help of sleeping tablets, because the only respite I got was in sleep. But if I woke in the night, that was it. I couldn't get back to sleep.

In February 2016, I accompanied my wife on a business trip to Peterborough, in England. We flew out and then travelled by train to Peterborough. It was a nightmare for me. The flight and the change in air pressure had caused all of my symptoms to greatly increase. I ended up in Peterborough City Hospital and we had to come home by train. A journey that had taken a few hours before, now took two days.

Back home, I was now starting to feel much worse. I contacted one of my doctors. Yes, so grand was I that I had now been appointed more than one! They explained what I already knew—that the plane flight had been a really bad idea. It had made everything much worse. So, now I knew I could no longer fly.

Things had gotten so bad for me, and I felt so terrible, that I would sit on the edge of the bed with my head in my hands moaning, "This can't go on!" I only went on because of Karen. But for her, I would not be here to write this.

During the following weeks, I would often say to Karen that I knew something was seriously wrong, but I didn't know what or what to do. I eventually went to my doctor, who immediately diagnosed clinical depression.

She put me on anti-depressants. I said I would try to keep working if I could. As I walked away, I phoned Karen, who was at work. But as I walked along the street in my town, I noticed people were looking at me strangely. I even said to Karen that people were looking at me. It was a few minutes before I realized why. I was crying! So it was now clear that I could not go to work.

The cloud was now directly overhead and blocking out everything!

It soon became clear I could not even be left alone. My amazing wife took a month unpaid leave to be with me. For the next month, I felt like a child that needed a baby sitter. I spent every minute with Karen. If she moved to another room, I would move with her. What my poor wife had to endure during those weeks....

During this time, one of my doctors had me fitted with a hearing aid that they assured me would help with the tinnitus. Now, I was just as skeptical about this as I suspect you are reading it. But it is true, it did! How? It has to do with what actually causes tinnitus. Over your lifetime, your brain gets used to receiving a certain level of sound from your ears. If that sound starts to reduce quickly, as it had with me, then your brain can "go looking" for the sound. If it doesn't find it, then sometimes it starts to produce its own sound. In a kind of way, it makes up for the missing sound. But this sound can be anything and it goes on 24/7. You see, you think the sound is coming from your ear, but it isn't. Your brain is producing it. Before this was understood, some people had their entire ear mechanism surgically removed. But it didn't help.

So! If your brain can be made to hear more sound, via a hearing aid, then it may stop producing this artificial sound, or at least reduce the volume.

It took a few months for this to work for me, because I had to slowly introduce myself to the hearing aid—increasing the time used each day until, after some weeks, I could use it all day.

Over a period of months, with the help of the anti-depressants and the hearing aid, I started to feel better. The tinnitus started to ease off, as did the hypersensitive eardrum. I didn't know then how long I would have to be on the anti-depressants. At the time of writing this, twenty months later, I am still on them, though I am slowly being weaned off. I hope that by the beginning of 2018, I may be off them entirely. The hypersensitive eardrum and tinnitus is still there as they always will be, but the tinnitus has significantly reduced in volume and has now changed to a steady electronic hum. I can live with it.

However, while the tinnitus and hypersensitive eardrum are much better, my other symptoms are still bad. I find travelling particularly difficult and likely to bring on seizures. Any level of stress will also do it.

One of the problems I have in getting people to understand my condition, is that I look fine on the surface. The only blatantly obvious, exterior sign that something is wrong is I now walk with a stick. One of the things people most often say, after I tell them about the tumor, is, "Well you look fine." I know they mean well, but I want to scream. On top of that, my condition itself is unusual and difficult to explain. My biggest problem is my balance, which is not good. When walking, I often stumble, wobble and find myself drifting off course. I have to concentrate to walk in a straight line. To anyone passing, I must look as if I am a little bit drunk.

The next thing they say is, "Can't you get treatment for it?" Explaining this is just as hard. You see, there are different types of surgeries you can get. But each carries with it potentially damaging side effects. They are not something you get done unless you have to. So I am in what is called "watch and wait."

Also, to be frank, like many people who have a major illness for a long time, I often get so fed up just talking about it.

***

In Britain, there is still a bad attitude among the general population towards disabled people. I have noticed so many times that if a disabled person is travelling along a street, people do not look at or acknowledge them. People don't want to get involved; they don't want to be bothered. They are afraid if they speak to someone in a wheelchair, the person might ask for help with something.

Many times in my life I have come to the aid of someone while everyone else just walked by. One day, I was walking through Belfast, where I worked, and in the distance I could see a man lying on the pavement, struggling to get up. As I walked towards him, I could see dozens of people walk past and ignore him. Now I don't care if he is just drunk, I will at least try to get him back on his feet so he can make it home safely. When I got up to this man, he was middle aged, well dressed and clearly sober. It transpired that he was disabled. He had fallen down on top of his crutch and couldn't get up. He was very upset and kept talking about how many people he had asked for help, as they had walked past, ignoring him.

I discovered this recently myself. My wife and I were walking home through a local car park and I had a seizure.

I couldn't walk or move. Karen managed to maneuver me a couple of paces to the side of the road, where I lay down. She then ran home for our car so she could get me home and into bed. As I lay there, dozens of people walked past and all made a pretense that they didn't even see me. I was well dressed and groomed, I had a walking stick, and I was clearly not drunk. Parents would even divert their children's gaze from me, teaching them young to ignore those in need of help. I must admit that this did upset me.

I have never been able to just walk past anyone in need, and still wouldn't today, despite my condition. If they are faking, then it is on them, not me. When Muhammad Ali was a very young man, he and a friend were walking along and Ali gave eight dollars to a beggar. As they continued, his friend started to berate Ali. How did he know if the man really needed money? He knew that Ali had only twelve dollars to his name. So now the beggar was richer than Ali. He thought Ali was being a fool. Ali smiled at him and replied that he had given the man the money with a pure heart. If the man were being dishonest, he would have to answer to God. That was all that mattered.

Many see the disabled as an inconvenience at best, and, at worst, I have heard many people express their anger that their hard-earned tax money goes towards supporting them. For example, I have often heard shop owners moan about the expense of having to build a simple wooden ramp at their shop entrance for people in wheelchairs, and taxi companies scream about having to make their vehicles accessible for the disabled.

Employers moan about having to accommodate disabled employees. In Britain, an employer doesn't have to go beyond what they deem as "reasonable" to accommodate them, and there is very little the person can do.

I would sum up the general attitude towards the disabled as being a non-contributory drain on society.

This attitude goes all the way to the top. Our current conservative government has recently changed the system for disabled support payments. Under this new system, the majority of people who were getting help have had it removed. Many are now homeless. Some have been forced to try to go back to work, and some have actually died while trying to work! Others have committed suicide and even the coroner's report cited the withdrawal of government support as a contributing factor.

I have worked for almost forty years and paid all my taxes. I have never claimed a penny from our government. In the last year, I have been turned down three times and have now been told I have to go to court to fight my case to try to get help.

Certainly, here in Britain, if you are disabled, you now have to fight harder than before for your rights and to get help.

Fortunately, my local authority is great. They organized a local home help group, which, when I'm bad, sends someone to check on me three times a day and make me something to eat. They also got a monitoring system installed that detects if I have fallen down, and if they can't get a response from me, they phone my wife. Before that, there were times she would come home to find me lying in a heap on the floor.

The town where I live has a high percentage of retirees, so all the local amenities are accessible to people who don't have full physical abilities. Nearly all of our shops and public places are wheelchair accessible, and we are fortunate our entire main street is flat, which makes it so much easier to travel on if you are in a wheelchair, or, like me, if you need to use a walking stick.

The local authority has purchased houses within existing developments for disabled people. These have support staffs that help the occupants. We have one of these in our own development.

With regards to my job, I was a computer programmer. I am now off work, because it was becoming very clear I simply couldn't get to work on anything like a regular basis. My biggest problem is travelling, and having to journey the thirty-plus miles each morning was causing me to have regular seizures at work. The first time it happened, the ambulance man said I would be better at home, as in hospital all I would be doing would be spending hours lying on a trolley in a corridor somewhere. Not only was this a nightmare for me, but also it interrupted several other people, as it took that many to get me out of the building and into our car. My wife would also have to leave her work, as I had to be taken home. Fortunately, my wife's employer is a rarity in that they are supportive and have not penalized her for those times. They have even allowed her to work a compressed week, so she can take each Friday off to drive me to my medical appointments.

I had been off sick for one hundred and twelve days in the previous twelve months. This had reached a point where, as my employer kept saying, it was "unsustainable." So I am now officially on an unpaid career break.

All of this means that, for the moment, I am a kept man. My wife has to work for both of us. But as a friend said, "Wouldn't it be worse if you had no one to keep you?"

Karen wakes at 5:30 a.m., and I get up with her and help her out to work, making breakfast and packing her lunch. I then get dressed and go for a walk. I'm supposed to walk daily to try to keep what's left of my balance going.

When back home, I have some tea and then spend most of my day at my computer. I break this up with housework, washing, and ironing. As my wife now has to work to keep us both, the least I can do is the housework, so she can come home to a tidy-ish house and a cooked meal.

So I am home alone. But I am not lonely. As Quentin Crisp said, "People are only lonely who don't know what to do with their time when they are alone." When I am feeling well enough, I can keep myself occupied; when not, I sit around moaning and feeling sorry for myself. My poor wife says I have become a great moaner. I could moan for Ireland at the Olympics. Well, if there were such a category, I'd give it a go. It would be nice to have a gold medal.

I know all this so far has been doom and gloom.

One thing that competitive sports teach you, is when you lose, you pick yourself up, try to figure out a way to improve, and give it another go. It is not just a matter of excelling physically; the best sportsmen also excel mentally. And yes, the time comes, for all sportsmen, when they can no longer compete. Then you find something else to do with your life.

And life takes such strange twists and turns. I have always thought it is not the big decisions we think we are making that change our lives, it is the little things we do, even without thinking, that have the biggest long-term effects. Turning right instead of left when you exit a street.

One seemingly small thing I did recently was let my beard grow. I have always had a beard, ever since leaving high school. It was always a short, trimmed beard, often a goatee. But then, in August 2016, I was going through a bad patch and shaving was difficult, so I decided to let it grow. To let it become a fine, big, manly beard! In fact, I ended up growing a "Yeard." Yes, a one years' growth of beard. This is a challenge that apparently all serious beardsmen must achieve once in their lives. I did it and then immediately trimmed it to half the length.

When I mention phrases like "beardsmen" or "bearded community," my wife laughs. So, as I type this, somewhere, she's having a good chuckle.

I started looking into beard grooming products. I purchased a few products and started using them. I liked one of them so much I did a YouTube video praising it. With no ulterior intentions, I sent the link for this video to the company—just to say how much I liked their product.

To my great surprise, they got in touch and asked me to review their other products. So they started sending me beard products, which I would use and then review on YouTube. Then, another beard company that had seen my videos contacted me. Soon, I was testing and reviewing products for three companies, then four.

Apparently, I must be good at this. I have been told by company reps that I am a very good communicator and very professional. Which is nice. I don't have an ego, but I can still appreciate a compliment.

Other companies started getting in touch with different products. My wife helps me with the testing, especially when the products are things like ladies head towels.

Soon, I found myself spending hours each day at this. There are days when I have nothing to test, but this is a nice break. Plus I'm not on a defined schedule, so if I'm not feeling up to it, I can take a day off.

I really enjoy this. It is entirely ad hoc. There is no contract, no financial reward; it is just an act of faith. Generally, they just send me the products and I test them. Of course, some products don't work, but that is the way of the world. I spent six months testing a new product for a beard company and it worked. In fact, it was great. But when they looked into the cost, they decided it was not viable.

Now I know this is not a career. But, I have known for the last two years—at over fifty, and with a debilitating brain tumor—my career was over anyway.

One other way I keep busy is by keeping in contact with my friends around the world.

I mentioned earlier that I am a published author. My first book was a biography of Quentin Crisp. For those of you who do not know who he was, have you heard of *The Naked Civil Servant*? Google him. The biography was published in 2009. When I was writing it, I met so many fascinating people. I met other writers, actors, artists, producers, directors, musicians, photographers, journalists and many more professionals. These people are distributed around the world, from the U.S. to South America, New Zealand, Japan, and Europe.

During the three years it took to write the book, I know I pestered them. But they never once refused or even delayed in answering my constant stream of questions. I knew, at the time, they were doing it for Quentin. One of them told me, "I would have done anything for Quentin when he was alive and I still would." Quentin died in 1999 at the age of ninety. I know how much I owe them all and that my book would be but a pale shadow of itself without their contributions.

As I got to know them, we became friends and I still keep in regular contact with them. They are such fascinating and talented people and so genuine and kind. It seems Quentin was attracted to these kinds of people and his legacy in friendships is now a great boon to me. They all enrich my life in ways that cannot be quantified, especially now that I cannot travel.

And of course I have my writing. I have a second novel to finish and I have ideas for several other books. I had wanted to do a biography of the actor Sir John Hurt. Anyone who knows enough about Quentin Crisp will also know that Sir

John played Quentin in the two biographical films about his life. *The Naked Civil Servant* in 1975 and *An Englishman in New York* in 2009. So it seemed to me the two books would make the perfect companion set.

I contacted Sir John (I had already been in touch with him about my Quentin Crisp biography), and he replied that he was interested. But, just weeks after, he was diagnosed with pancreatic cancer. Around the same time, I also started having real problems with my own health. And now, very sadly, the great man has left us. Sir John died in January 2017. I still hold out hope that I might do the book posthumously.

During the last two years I have rediscovered what is really important to me. Things like your job, while important, are not your life—at least not for me. Yes, I enjoyed my work, and my work colleagues, and I count myself lucky there. Yes, I studied for many years to get to where I was. I did my first computer course in 1987. I'm an honors graduate, and I have so many qualifications I can't remember them all. Yet, in spite of all that, I have always worked to live, not lived to work.

For now, I value each day more than I can say. I also value each minute I spend with my wife and with my friends. Life is the richer for it, and every experience more rewarding. Now that I am no longer working, sometimes days and even weeks can go by without an attack. So generally I am feeling more stable.

So while the dark cloud is still over me, it is not as solid. I can see sunlight through it.

I have discovered I am stronger than I thought, though I think a lot of that strength comes from having Karen in my life. She inspires me and, to paraphrase Jack Nicholson in *As Good As It Gets*, she makes me want to be a better person.

A friend on Facebook recently put up a post that said, "You don't know how strong you are until strong is all there is left to be."

Landmines

Caitlin Hernandez

When he and I met, I don't recall feeling a spark. I liked him, but in a vague, absentminded way.

The first time we walked together, I shyly grasped his elbow, and he led me into an elevator, then to a chair. He was sweet and solicitous—his warmth and good intentions were as unmistakable as his audible smile—but he seemed so polite and put-together that I never imagined we'd become close friends.

As time passed, we shared words and music, moving more and more quickly toward common ground. I found myself becoming drawn to him, inexorably. A pulsing, joyous energy radiated from his voice, and spirit, and gentle hands. His easy openness inspired closeness, and I took to needlessly tucking my arm in his whenever we stood side by side.

I liked to imagine that his kindness and creativity and raucous laughter lit up his face, making his dark eyes dance. But I also sensed, in him, a deep well of sadness: silently screaming pain. I could hear it throbbing behind his smile, feel it vibrating beneath his warm, smooth skin. My hands and heart and empathy, readying to fight for him, suddenly seemed inadequate and ineffectual.

I began to fall for him, I think, on the day he demonstrated his understanding that, in order to feel seen, I needed to be touched. My hands were occupied on the piano keys, and I was seated, so instead of hugging me hello, he greeted me and placed an unassuming hand on my shoulder. I stopped playing long enough to cover his hand with mine, and for a heartbeat, we stayed like that: his palm cupping my shoulder, my fingers crisscrossing his longer ones, and the song I'd written on pause. The only thing I could truly see was the blazing overhead fluorescents, but I swore I could feel his affectionate gaze.

I doubt he remembers that. Most people don't remember those moments: the exchanges that mean so little to them, but are everything to me.

Time continued to pass, and he and I became still closer. By that point, I could gauge there was much more going on inside him than I was able to understand. I couldn't help worrying, but I also accepted that, outside of being a good friend, there was almost certainly nothing I could do for him. Still, he was never far from my thoughts. Never, in all my life, had I been shaken by such an overpowering need to become close to someone.

I strapped his name and his spirit to my 11:11 wishes, sending them sailing into the sea again and again. They were my starfish: my "Starlight, star bright, first star I see tonight." I alternated wishes: safety for him and his loved ones, his happiness, his goals, and his dreams.

He himself mattered so much more to me than my own wistful wish that, one day, he might notice me longing to mean something to him.

The hopelessness of the situation was, to my mind, absolute. We'd each loved both men and women, but I'd been with more women and he'd been with more men. He was excited and carefree about love; I was frightened and cautious. He was as accepting of my blindness as it was possible to be, but I couldn't help thinking, although I knew it was unfair and untrue, that my being totally blind had effectively erased me from whatever list of desirable people he may have been keeping.

I acknowledged, though I didn't want to, that he and I were unlikely ever to be anything other than friends. If I were lucky, we'd be good friends. But hoping for anything more was foolish.

The first time he kissed me, he wasn't entirely sober, but I was. We were with friends, singing and dancing along to music. Some people were taking shots of whiskey, but I'd had only one. I'd been beside him all day; I was happy enough without alcohol.

I was surrounded by enough loved ones that I felt safe without my cane. Perhaps noticing its absence, he draped his arms over my shoulders to shield me from the crowd, carefully arranging his hands beneath my chin.

I trusted few boys, but he was certainly one of those few. Still, past experiences spoke more loudly than trust, and I reflexively closed my hands over his, just in case.

Immediately, he began to pull away—to apologize, to ask if I was okay—but I tightened my hands over his and told him the truth: that I loved this. The last thing I wanted was for him to let go.

We stayed like that, my cheek brushing the softness of his dress shirt, his hands warm and gentle across my collarbone.

Later that night, he put a hand on my shoulder—accustoming me to his touch, as always—before curving his piano fingers across my cheek and asking, "May I?"

It meant the entire world to me that he asked. So few others had cared about what I wanted.

I must have nodded or shrugged or smiled—something affirmative—because he leaned in and touched his lips to mine. Even though I'd known what was coming, I was so surprised that I didn't have time to kiss him back. I'd also forgotten that, unlike women and high school boys, men might have beards. The unexpected tickle made me giggle, and he laughed, too, for reasons I could only guess at.

We spontaneously turned the kiss into a hug, and my heart soared. I'd craved that kiss for so long.

The next day, I invited him over. My mind was teeming with questions; I needed to know what page he was on so I could turn my own pages accordingly.

My hands were shaking so much as I made him tea that I'm sure I must have dropped one or two lemon seeds into his cup. If I did—if I appeared to be nervous or uneasy—he didn't comment or rush in to help, and I loved him for that.

I asked him if he remembered the night before. He admitted that—yes—he did. He sounded sheepish, almost guilty, and I hastened to assure him that I hadn't minded, that everything was fine.

"Oh, good," he exhaled in relief. "It just seemed like the right thing to do in that moment."

I curled in to him on the couch, needing to know that we were okay. He didn't respond. In front of our friends, he and I were always hugging, always holding hands. We were never not touching. But when we were alone together, he only ever reached out when my blindness demanded helping hands. I'd always wondered about that, and now I wondered with even greater insistence.

Months flew by. I waited: for him to kiss me again, for him to bring up that night, for him to treat me the slightest bit differently. He never did.

By June, when we were both slated to go to a friend's concert, I'd long since discarded any and every expectation. I didn't wear anything special that night, didn't give my hair an extra comb. I wasn't even sure he would be there.

He was. When I heard his voice, I sprang to my feet and, not bothering to unfold my cane, flailed in his direction. He caught me in his arms, and we laughed as we hugged.

I babbled into the coarse material of his jacket, "I've missed you . . . it's been so long . . . how are you?"

He disengaged from the embrace, leaving his hands on my arms. "How are you?"

I raised my eyebrows. "I just asked you that."

He laughed, squeezing me playfully around the shoulders. "Honestly, I couldn't catch a word; I just heard a bunch of happy mumbling."

I giggled and teetered up on tiptoes to hug him again. Obligingly, he bent down, and we met in the middle, swaying absently in each other's arms.

Nobody in the world could hold me the way he could: at once gently and strongly, unassumingly and confidently. I drank in the feeling: his smooth cheek and strong chest on mine; his arms around my waist; his open hands painting circles on my back; his long, heavy hair framing our faces; the smell of his skin, clean and crisp and woodsy.

Standing in front of him, my head on his chest as he held me close, I felt pleasantly small and protected. Touching and being touched by him rekindled the dregs of dormant hope, warming me from skin to soul.

He jokingly led me to a chair behind a pillar—"I figured you wouldn't mind taking one for the team and filling the seat with no view"—and bought me macaroni and cheese. We shared it, spoons colliding, shoulders joggling. He held my hand reasonlessly atop the table, the way he so often did. He waited with me in the bathroom line so I wouldn't have to use my cane, and I leaned into his shoulder as he wrapped his arm behind my back. But we were friends. I didn't think anything of any of it . . . or, at least, I told myself not to.

Later, long after our friends had left, we playfully danced . . . and somewhere between my third and fourth alternating chocolate cake and Fireball shots, he kissed me again. This time, I rallied and kissed him in return.

He tasted like chocolate and cinnamon and the orange juice I'd insisted on adding to my last Fireball to make it less alcoholic. Kissing him felt, in every way, like Christmas, like a blend of thrills and eagerness and wild joy.

My intensity must have alarmed him; I remember him pulling back, gently guiding my head onto his shoulder, and hugging me as he said, "It's okay, love . . . I'm still the same person."

I knew that . . . but I wasn't the same person.

Emboldened as much by the shots as by the magical turn the night had taken, I confessed that I had feelings for him. His responses were as much honest as ambiguous.

"Ever since we met, I've had the deepest respect for you," he said. "I'm so blessed to know you."

"I want all sorts of amazing things to happen for you," he said, "and they will. I have no doubt that you'll meet and love many wonderful people. And if I can be one of those people, then all the better for me."

I asked him if he didn't think it was odd—two queer souls colliding and connecting the way ours were doing—and he replied, "I think it's beautiful. Love is love, Caitlin. I've always loved you . . . and I'm attracted to you. We could absolutely work. You're a remarkable, giving person. You're beautiful, inside and out."

I couldn't not believe him.

Later, once the shots' kick had dwindled to a negligible, giddy buzz, he escorted me home. We sang for our Uber driver, and I nestled my hand between his, pressing my nose against the cold window and watching the San Francisco streetlights flash past.

At my building, I put my arm in his and led him upstairs. I asked, timidly, if we could leave the lights off. When he said of course, I knew that, finally, if only for a moment, he and I had turned to the same page.

I'd led only a small handful of people to this point. Few had lived up to my expectations, and because of that, I was both elated and frightened by his presence, by the question of how he would fare on my rutted, uneven terrain.

Taking his hands in mine, I towed him to my couch, pried off his zip-up boots, carefully removed his glasses, and asked him what he could see.

"Just the moonlight, really." As ever, he seemed unfazed, both by my actions and my question. "And the outlines of the window frames."

That was fair enough; all I could feel was the heat furling around the edges of what could be, what might be.

I clambered into his lap and kissed him, rapturously . . . and he kissed me back. He did.

He kissed and touched me in a way no boy ever had: eagerly, but also protectively, compassionately. Each of his steps forward traveled on an inhale; my consent yielded the corresponding exhale. So much emotion sizzled between us—mine, certainly, but I thought his as well—and my every molecule quivered.

It was all so new, so unexpected . . . and yet his sensitivity struck a familiar, lulling chord.

I needed him to think I was brave and competent and capable, and I struggled, in those blissful, breathless minutes, to be all those things. But a prickly tangle of thorns persisted in choking me. Almost every time someone had seen me this way—almost every time I'd trusted anyone this much—disaster had followed. I couldn't help being wary, guarded, and unsure. But if I couldn't trust him to do this right, then I couldn't trust anyone.

Only three other boys had ever come this close to me, and only one of them had done at all well.

I'd led the first boy, taking his hand to balance him as he tiptoed over the stepping stones. He had done everything right, in spite or perhaps because of the undeniable truth dividing us. He couldn't love me in the same way I loved him.

Before he left, he planted scores of carnations, my favorite flowers. To this day, whenever I cry, their petals brush my cheeks, soothing me, reminding me of adolescence, and innocence, and the sweet, simple selflessness that love should always contain. When I see that boy now, he always takes the time to kneel beside the carnations, caressing their petals between his thumbs and forefingers.

The second boy had never been invited past the walkway. He came anyway, kicking aside the stepping stones, pushing through my scrupulously placed defenses—my familiar landmarks. He brazenly trampled the carnations and shattered the greenhouse's fragile glass panes. He destroyed almost everything before sneaking away without a word.

After him, my skin was a layer or two thinner. My first love's carnations bent double, damaged stalks threatening to snap under the power of furious, whipping winds. Touches, even the most well meaning, scalded. I alternately sniped at those who claimed to understand, swatted at hands that tried to piece me back together, and scoffed at those who, for whatever reason, could not or would not listen.

The third boy was equipped with ten years' knowledge of who I was; he confidently navigated the stepping stones dividing his world from mine. He should have reorganized the cluttered walkway, swept up the broken glass, watered the carnations. He was able to do all that—he knew it was necessary—but he chose not to.

In the wake of his impulsiveness, weeds grew up between the stones. The countless glass shards became still more lethal and jagged as they fractured underfoot. The carnations began wilting, delicate petals crumbling into dust.

Even now, years later, his betrayal, unintentional though it was, still lives inside my chest: a rough-edged rubber band that loosens only when I'm safe. Whenever it contracts, I think of him: that third boy, who knew better but didn't care enough to make the right choice.

No boy approached the stepping stones after those three. Had any boy dared to try, I would have sent him scrambling. I was busy trying, mostly futilely, to rebuild.

It fell to my first female lover to patch my wounds, and she bravely, gracefully rose to the challenge. Whenever she touched me, she let my hands hover over hers. Knowing that speech might fail me at crucial moments, she held me only in light, watching my face, honing her awareness to match mine.

She was as much cautious as caring; she focused on what I needed rather than what she wanted. Patience and empathy imbued her hands with love: so much love that my very blood seemed to sing with it. With her bare fingertips, she picked up each and every splinter of glass. She smoothed the disturbed pathways with her palms and planted fragrant eucalyptus everywhere. Chunks of glass were still missing from several of the greenhouse's panes—large, irreplaceable pieces that were obviously, visibly absent—and she covered the cracks as best she could with trellises of jasmine.

Ultimately, she left . . . but by then, I was a newer, stronger person. The girl who came after her set the jasmine shuddering and the scent of eucalyptus fading . . . but I was able to make repairs without help. The seeds my first two loves had sewn were living proof that I deserved better.

And now, six years after the last boy, here I was with the first man.

He was doing well: leaving the stepping stones in place, gently touching the carnations' petals, breathing in the jasmine, meticulously gathering fallen eucalyptus pods. He was healing me as much with touch as with the time he took and the things he chose not to try. He handled me as though I was spun glass, but more as though I was something precious than something breakable.

Even as the memories of brokenness scraped my heels, the redolence of carnations and eucalyptus and jasmine floated through my head. I wanted to move forward, but was too anxious to do so . . . and knew enough to understand that.

Tentatively, I slid my hands inside his crisp, long-sleeved shirt, leaving him to unfasten his belt and kick off his jeans. He lay back, hands resting, open and unmoving, at his sides. He let me discover, but only what and when and if I wanted. He didn't expect or insinuate or even suggest, and his patient stillness was my security. There would be no surprises, no predetermined endpoints or finish lines or outcomes. Whether he was determining my needs instinctively or by educated guessing, I didn't know . . . but his silent promise was exactly what I needed.

His lips stayed on mine—we didn't say much—but his hands, gliding slowly across my skin, spoke to me as clearly as if words were spilling from his fingertips: "Relax. This is for you—all for you—and that is completely okay. You need this—you deserve it—and you're safe with me. Remember what I said before: We could work. We could absolutely work. This is our beginning. We have time."

When he and I stalled at an impasse, words tripped past my kiss-numbed lips: "I'm kind of scared."

"Don't be." He drew me in close, arranging his arm over my hip in such a way that his hand built a barrier between his skin and mine. "Nothing is going to happen that you don't want to happen. We'll do whatever you want and nothing more."

I rested my head against his shoulder. "I feel stupid."

"Caitlin, don't." He said it at once softly and intensely as he rubbed my bare back. "Don't at all. You're fine."

Intimacy alone is powerful enough to erase blindness, albeit temporarily. In darkness, with only touch, trust, and a handful of words, he and I were equals, and the bittersweet novelty of it all wrapped my heart like a silken vise.

For the first time in my twenty-five years, I felt not only wanted, but also chosen: spontaneously and completely, without questions or complications. For the first time, I felt happiness and safety and joy in being seen.

I remember thinking that, if only things were different—if only I were different—I might have known this rite of passage much sooner. And I remember wondering, fleetingly but vividly, whether he wished he could look at me here, in the darkness he'd willingly stepped into: my darkness, which we now shared. I myself longed only to know whether his face would have told me anything important, whether his eyes were as soft and fluid and open as his hands.

What we were doing—or, rather, not doing—must have seemed pathetic to him. I'd relegated him to Little League after he'd been playing in the Majors for years. But the slow, purposeful tenderness in his arms and lips and fingers washed away my doubt and guilt and shame in a heady rush of blood.

Overwhelmed, I white-knuckled the edge of a chasm, seeking and not finding the wherewithal either to leap across or step back. I was unraveling from the outside in, unable to speak. All I could do was scrabble for his hand, for an anchor, for something to keep me from either crying or crashing.

Most people miss the moments when I freeze, when my emotions get the best of me, when I need something but am too overwrought to frame that request in words. But—it was like magic—at the exact instant I needed it, his hand materialized, clasping mine with fierce, heartfelt assurance. In a way nothing else could have done, his touch reminded me who he was, whose singular, long-desired essence was seeping into my system. He squeezed my hand and, together, we vaulted over the abyss.

Afterward, I drew him up along my body and we kissed as I fought back poignant tears. He had restored my faith, not just in other people, but also in myself. But there simply weren't enough words in the world to express that to him. And I was also aware—sharply, painfully aware—that this could very well be my only chance, not just with him, but also with anyone like him. Words might ruin everything.

During those peaceful, pre-dawn hours after he left, my happiness was almost agonizingly exquisite. Haltingly, disbelievingly, I traced each thread of the memory: every fragile, flawless stitch of us. I thought that maybe—just maybe—I'd finally made a good decision: a safe, strong, sweet decision that wouldn't slip through my fingers before I was ready to let it go.

I clung to and internalized every intricacy: his warm, unfaltering attentiveness; the firm precision in his words and his hands; the strength of character he'd demonstrated by calmly, quietly, humbly meeting me exactly where I was, never nudging me even a single step farther forward. Just as he'd promised, we'd done only what I wanted, nothing more. His kindness and generosity moved me so deeply that I felt as though my heart was being shredded.

He'd cared more about what I needed than what he wanted. I wasn't used to that brand of sacrifice, of respect. In a way, I'd never known it.

As light filled my windows, I felt, by turns, dazed and delighted, overjoyed and overcome. Tiny flickers of hope flamed to life inside me, overriding the other emotions. A river of something indefinable—something pure and sweet as sunshine—was tingling through my core. Suddenly, inexplicably, I could breathe more easily. My skin, though still frayed and threadbare in places, embraced me in a way it hadn't since I was a child.

I'd taken a chance—a wild, graceless leap off a long-feared precipice—and not only was I intact, I was better for having leapt.

In many ways, I'm perceptive. I notice and remember small specifics and seemingly irrelevant details. In spite or perhaps because of my blindness, I can often see the big picture with vivid clarity. But in other ways, I am simply blind, unable—or perhaps just unwilling—to see what's right in front of me.

I never, ever thought he would walk away. But that morning, and that week, and the next week, and the next month . . . he and I didn't talk about it.

We danced around the subject. I was shy, and he, I surmised, was wary.

When I finally wrote to him, his reply managed, somehow, to address what had happened while avoiding the nuts and bolts of that night: "I love you, but I'm not in love with you."

His response was disappointing, but not devastating. I understood and accepted what he was saying . . . but still, I needed something more. Whether or not he knew it, our shared year had made him one of my very best friends. He and I weren't two strangers who had stumbled home together. I needed him, in the aftermath of that night, to treat my soul with as much consideration as he had my skin.

Try though I had to forget, I still felt empty and gutted months later. His touch had left a sentient imprint: warm and electric, breathing and boiling and buzzing in my bones. Some days, it burned. My skin was beginning to fray again. The sunshine he'd left behind was dulling to gray.

I wrote to him once more, asking if we could talk. He said of course. Of course he said of course.

He picked me up a little late, hugged me unhesitatingly, and told me my new short haircut was beautiful. He cut my chicken so I wouldn't have to. He held doors and chairs and my hand. Leaving the restaurant, I held my rainbow-colored cane in one hand, his hand in my other. Halfway across a street, a man shouted, jubilantly and genuinely, from the preceding block, "You two are so cute! I love it!"

He and I both laughed. When I squeezed his hand, he squeezed back.

We passed the music store near my place, and I begged him to play. At first, I sat beside him on the piano bench, listening . . . but that wasn't enough. I needed, desperately, to be close to him.

Leaning my upper body behind his, I aligned our arms and covered his hands with mine: lightly, so as not to impede his playing, but determinedly enough that I could "watch." He turned his head—he didn't need to watch his hands to play perfectly—and just as I had a year before, when we were together at another piano, I sensed his gaze. His smile was only a shade away from being soundless—a minute exhale, not even half a breath --but it shimmered in the air between us, twinkling like invisible starlight on my skin and in my eyes.

I was only ever able to see starlight in wintry darkness: a splash of vital warmth in a sea of numbing coldness.

Resting my forehead against his shoulder blade, I closed my eyes tightly, struggling against tears. I followed his flying fingers, my airy touch shadowing his fervent one. His crystalline notes spun a web around us; my bones sparkled.

I remembered that, when he made or heard music, he saw colors. Maybe that was why he could see me so much more clearly than most other people were able to. (Although, he didn't seem to see my heart aching and breaking against his back.)

Later, we sat on my couch—that same couch—with what felt like yards of space between us. I told him how I felt and why, and he listened.

"I need this to not happen again." It was hard to dislodge the words from my chalky throat. "And you have to do that. Because I can't trust myself."

"I hear that." He said it solemnly, understandingly.

I leaned in to him, but he didn't reach back.

The last thing I wanted—the last thing I'd meant to request—was for him to pull away from our friendship, to build a barrier between us. I knew, already, that was what he intended to do, and my blood began to feel like frozen fire, like a scream, like knives under my skin. I would have snatched back my words and crushed them into smithereens in a heartbeat, if only that meant he would hold me.

I needed him to touch me meaningfully enough that I'd feel seen again, the way I had when we'd kissed and held each other in darkness. I needed him to tell me that night hadn't been a meaningless mistake. I needed him to insist he didn't regret it. I needed him to appreciate how much it had cost me to let him in at all: to open up to and trust him, even though others—boys who were not so unlike him—had given me every reason to deadbolt my doors indefinitely.

I needed him to know, for better or worse, I had loved him with my whole heart. To a degree, I still did.

I'd run out of strength, words, and courage. The small piece of us he'd left behind was stabbing my throat and carving holes inside my chest. It was hard to breathe and even harder not to cry.

I sensed he felt my anguish, but couldn't trace it to its root. He left without kissing my cheek the way he so often had, and I couldn't have felt more lost if I'd been abandoned in a forest.

I'd been nothing but honest with him, perhaps to a fault . . . and maybe it was asking too much to expect the same unfiltered honesty in return.

So much of who I am—queerness, and blindness, and the knotted, messy masses in between—is sequestered in silence, relegated to a place where even I sometimes lose sight of it. My first two lovers had loved me in that silence, only to leave me there, alone. I'd needed—I'd ached—for him to be different. His staying would have made all the difference.

My first young love—the first boy—left carnations to remind me. My first adult love—the first girl—left eucalyptus and jasmine to guide and protect me. I'm not sure what he, the first man, left as his legacy. If he did leave something, I don't know what purpose the offering might serve.

I'm not proud of some of the thoughts I had, afterward, when I was tasked with reconfiguring the disassembled facets of myself.

If those two boys who'd come before him hadn't left me so scared and so scarred—if I'd been bold enough to do more for him, if I'd given him a good, compelling reason to come back, rather than a million reasons to run—would he have stayed?

If I were more talented, less open, more or less feminine or masculine, would he have stayed? If I were taller than five feet, if I was still stick-thin and proud of my figure the way I was in high school, if my dark eyes weren't partially clouded, if I could make eye contact and flirt and wear all the "right" clothes, would he have stayed?

If he could have looked into my eyes, might he have seen how and what I felt for and about him? And if he had seen some or all of that, would it have mattered to him?

If I could see, might he have stayed?

And why?

Why did any of it happen in the first place?

Had he simply recited those words—"We could work"—in the same way one fits a key in a lock: automatically, unthinkingly, only as a means of opening an otherwise impenetrable door? Or had it truly been a mistake: a slip of the tongue amplified by liquid courage.

I would never want to erase what happened between us. But if he was going to walk away—and he must have known all along that he would—I almost wish he'd left me alone, where I was.

Almost.

It wasn't fair of him to take my hand and start a journey with me, only to change heart halfway and leave me among landmines. I forgave him for leaving even before he was gone, but I wished, so much, he had guided me to the foot of the trail, where the carnation petals would whisper beneath my bare feet, the jasmine would flutter through my open hands, the eucalyptus would cleanse my dry lungs as I ventured, alone, back through the maze of stepping stones.

I daydream, sometimes, that he and I will meet again, ten years from now. Maybe I'll have a partner, maybe a couple kids. He probably will, too. Maybe, after we catch up—after I hug his partner and he hugs mine, after the little ones have been introduced, after everyone has small-talked in a chatty bunch—we'll go for pizza. The kids will play with the vending machines and video games, helping each other and trading prizes, while we adults discuss music lessons and soccer games and the PTA and the outrageous cost of living. He and my partner will both move, in reflexive concert, to refill my soda, pass me extra napkins, give me their croutons before I have time to ask. All four of us will laugh.

***

Later, our partners will round up the brood for playtime at the park so he and I have a chance to reminisce.

He and I will walk together the way we always did: side by side, his warm, long-fingered hand entirely enveloping my cold one. We'll find a café and order: coffee with cream and sugar for him, chocolate milk for me, the way it always was. He'll choose an outdoor bench and we'll sit together—just close enough for our shoulders and knees to companionably touch—because almost from the beginning, that was our way of connecting, of looking into each other's eyes and smiling.

After an hour or so—after old friends and old stories have been recounted—maybe I'll bring up that night. The conversation might be easy, brief, and lighthearted. He might answer my questions without my needing to ask them. He might loop an arm around me in an absentminded side-hug, and we'll both chuckle with indulgent self-deprecation.

Or maybe the conversation will be slower, longer, dotted with pensive pauses and stoic silences. I might rest my head on his shoulder, and he might tell me that, ten years ago, he wanted to reach out—to talk and listen to and help me— but couldn't think how to do it. Maybe he'll wrap his strong, steady fingers around my hand, squeeze, and tell me he's sorry. His apology won't be necessary—not anymore—but it will still matter more than he'll know, and I'll still appreciate and thank him for it.

Finally, we'll walk back to the park, arm-in-arm. We'll gather the gang, our hands—his powerful but intuitive, mine small but discerning—stringing together a chain of our loves, with us and our history as the focal point.

I'm sure he'll hug me goodbye the way he did before everything changed: firmly and affectionately and unhesitatingly, rubbing my back and kissing my cheek. I'm sure he'll hold on for one more sequence of heartbeats, because he'll know I want and need him to. The elapsed years will weave a cloud-mist canopy above and around us: invisible to the eye, but pleasantly cool and refreshing on our skin, like a memory of dancing sea foam. Our old songs will loiter sweetly in the corners of our consciousness, crescendoing occasionally only to recede to a lulling hum.

Overdubbing the Cody Effect

Sam E. Rubin

I was two and a half or so. Naked, always naked, but draped in a soft pashmina shawl, well, a shawl ripped to shreds by the two and a half years of my clutching to it, feeling its softness on my skin. I called it Binkie. Draped over my shoulders, Binkie and I stood in front of a little portable TV with a tape deck.

On the tape, virtuoso violinist Nigel Kennedy played Vivaldi's "Four Seasons." In one arm, I held a small violin. In the other, a cello bow, because it actually made sound. Compared to a violin bow the same size, it had a wider swath of horse hair.

The little TV that played the tape of Nigel sat on a small table in a playroom that my family called the Cozy Room—a turret-shaped room, overlooking a courtyard of plum trees, behind a house on College Avenue in Berkeley, California. The house, we were told by an aging hippie who showed up at the door one day, had been a meeting place for the Free Speech Movement back in the sixties.

Nigel and I played "Four Seasons" together over and over and over and over. It was one of the great joys of my life, giving me endless hours of happiness. I could feel the electrifying zing of his music jiggling the molecules of my body. When the last measure of the last season of the piece came, Nigel and I held that final note. The vibration of it hung mid-air between up and down, in and out, the apex between the in-breath and the out-breath, between sensation and stillness. I can still remember all this—Binkie over my shoulders, the dark walls of the hippie house, plum blossoms softly falling off the trees outside, Nigel's virtuoso violin.

The house was located next to the Julia Morgan Theater, which hosted all kinds of musical and theatrical events. It was like living in the practice room next to the other practice rooms behind the stage. The magic of theater and performance constantly filled the air. And I, on my little stage in the Cozy Room, played one-on-one with one of the Greats. I wasn't exactly playing violin, of course. I just mimicked Nigel, bowing wildly or softly, depending on the movement –"Spring," "Summer," "Fall," "Winter"—the energy of the music coursing through my body. It so moved me and I had to move with it. Life was good, free, and beautiful.

My mother recounts a story from around that time. She and my dad and I were at a local restaurant. I pointed out music playing on speakers in the background. They said they couldn't hear it. "Vivaldi!" I said, too loud, not in my restaurant voice. Of course, it was Vivaldi. I could have picked Vivaldi out in a tornado. And Wieniawski. And Paganini. And Donizetti. You get the point. They asked the waiter because they really could not hear the music. He said, "Yes, it's violin music. We keep it low in the background."

Sometime between this magical world and age four, everything started to bother my hearing and I, also, stopped talking. At first, my parents say they chalked it up to me obviously being a musician. "Musicians don't talk much," my mother told the teacher when they confronted her with my silence. But, my preschool urged them to get me tested because they said something had "gone terribly wrong" with me. From their perspective, there was a moment where everything changed with me. I think everyone saw it, but the school was the first to point it out. Eventually, I did get tested.

The results of the test: High-Functioning Autism (HFA). It felt like falling into an abyss, a void of darkness where I could see the people I was drifting away from, but I had no control over my body, and no way to get out or to speak to reach them. I was simply in another space, a different universe, falling perceptibly farther and farther from them, even while being in the presence of others. It left me in a trapped, imprisoned void, unable to get out, unable to find words I once had, and completely at the mercy of others.

My parents report the experience of my becoming autistic as watching me drown and not being able to catch me. So, I think we were all confused by the change in me. And, in a way, we all fell into the depths of the vortex that was sucking me further and further from the simple happiness of childhood. "Away" is probably the best word to describe it, because I was there and not there at the same time—like a one-way mirror. And things changed in every way for me.

Auditory sensations were acute. My visual field presented me with what I would now characterize as trails. People's faces phase-shifted. My mother had four eyes. Binkie still gave me some comfort, but I could feel a kind of scratchiness I had not formerly experienced. It was as if the weight of life suddenly pressed in on me, so much so that even my beloved blanket became an irritation.

Thus ended my Cozy Room days. I was thrust into special education. I will credit my teacher for helping me get words back. But her methodology was not gentle. We were a motley crew of mismatched four-year-olds with a variety of neurological and possibly psychological disabilities, from autism to spasticity to selective mutism to oppositional defiance disorder. There were about a dozen of us; I don't remember exactly. What I do remember is the terror of being in a special education class.

On a typical day, some of my classmates would climb the shelves with the teacher and aides, at first, coaxing them down, and then, threatening them with punishment if they didn't come down. One boy was left to cry himself out in the corner. Another boy was just confused, I think, because he never could stay in one place for more than a minute. I think, for each of us, our inner intelligence was compelling us to try to escape. I was too freaked out to go against the rules. I saw what happened to the climbers and the screamers, the biters, and the kickers. They would get tied to chairs or an aide would sit on them to calm them down.

Circle time was about trying to speak. The teacher would herd us together and sing, "Where's Sam Rubin? Where's Sam Rubin?" She encouraged me to say, "Here I am." Eventually, the words came. And then, more words. But, I wasn't always able to pay attention, because I was distracted by the boy who was left in the corner to cry. I was worried about the kid tied to the chair (which I called the Lonely Chair), because he was flipping out, trying to break free from his imprisonment. When my attention wandered to the obvious distractions, the teacher would bark my name to get me to look at her. If I didn't respond (I did have auditory-processing issues, so sometimes it took a few seconds for my name to register on my brain), I'd get whacked across the face to "pay attention" in circle. Or she'd grab my face to point it to look at her. And, one time, she yanked my legs because I wasn't sitting cross-legged. I fell back and hit my head. Being in that class was frightening and in my little four-year-old mind, I certainly didn't want to end up in the Lonely Chair. I started to live in fear of making mistakes. This set up a pattern that has dogged me since.

It just takes one mean teacher to leave an indelible scar. In my case, the first one was bad enough. But, it was my fourth grade teacher, Cody, who really seared abject fear into the fabric of my being. He was beyond strict. It felt as if he was constantly looking over every student, like a bird of prey, waiting for the student to make a mistake, so he could punish him or her with writing lines on a piece of paper.

Now, this may not sound too bad, especially when you compare it to being locked in a closet or tied to a chair in order to "behave," but it was very difficult for me to hold a pencil, painful even. It was difficult to feel the sensation of my fingers on the pencil and to control it. This had to do with some aspect of the neurological sensory motor damage I had endured that got me the autism diagnosis.

With Cody, for the slightest infraction, I had to stay inside from playground and write lines. For me, this was torture. I wanted to run around on the playground. I needed to run around, move my body. But, in the World According to Cody, classroom discipline prevailed. Playground was held hostage to make the students behave. This was his power trip.

Whereas, at home, my parents were constantly celebrating the fact that I could finally talk again, refraining from talking in a classroom was an entirely different matter. It didn't help that I was the archetype of the classroom comic. I couldn't help myself. I had to comment on everything. It was like hiccups; the words just erped out of my mouth. A typical line for me to have to write in Cody's class was: "I will not talk during class."

The contrast between my world at home and the world at school was not lost on me. At home, my sense of self-worth and worthiness were nurtured. At school, this was shut down. I don't see this as a malicious thing. It's just a function of the special education environment, which is structured through the lens of behavioral intervention. If you could behave, which meant sitting quietly in a chair at a desk, that was somehow construed to mean you were actually learning something.

Remember the film *Chappie*, by South African director Neil Bloomkamp? Chappie was a robot that was gifted by his creator with consciousness. But, he fell into the wrong hands and the people he was with, as well meaning as they thought they were being, were actually quite cruel to him. They did things to him that were physically painful to him. He was learning, but he wasn't learning the things that would make him into a socially appropriate humanoid robot. As a child robot, he was so sincere. He kept trying to please his tormentors, just as a student tries to please his teacher. In special ed, I was Chappie. Cody was my tormentor.

One day, in Cody's class, I was trying to inch my chair forward, closer to my desk, while doing a math test. I accidentally bumped a student with my knee. The student reacted and said, "You kicked me." Then, he told the teacher that I had kicked him. Without asking my side of the story, Cody immediately jumped on the alleged infraction and tasked me with lines: "Alright Sam!!! You owe a page of lines!!!" I was so upset at the unfairness of it that I failed the math test that day. This cycle repeated itself in many different ways on different days: If I talked without raising my hand, I would owe a page of lines. If I counted on my fingers to get an answer for a math test, I would owe a page of lines. At some point, I became so fearful of making a mistake, particularly in math, that anything having to do with math ended up being an extremely traumatic experience for me.

One day, during a test, I held the math flash cards up to the sun so I could see the answers on the other side. I zoomed through the test. I couldn't wait to get out to the playground. Of course, Cody took me to task on this. Lines. More lines.

When I told my mother, she said, "You cheated. Wow!" To her, this meant I had the awareness to cheat, which to her meant I was recovering from autism. She had the same positive reaction the first time I lied to her. "You lied! Wow!" Don't get me wrong. She did take the time to explain why what I did was wrong and socially uncool, but she praised me for my range of responses to a challenging situation.

From the conditioning I received from Cody's class, math became a source of trauma. I developed a belief I wasn't good in math. As a result, I simply stopped trying. Not only did I stop trying, but I also devised an elaborate set of behaviors to resist math at every turn, including a severe itch that would come over me when it was time for math. Sometimes, I would scratch myself to the point of bleeding. This would ensure no one would force me to do math. Of course, that wasn't going to fly with my mom. In her mind, if I could lie and cheat, I was clever enough to figure out how to do math.

Because I spent all my time just coping, I wasn't learning much. I was about to enter sixth grade and was functionally illiterate. I could barely count. I couldn't add, subtract, multiply, or divide. I could barely read. At that point, I was in perpetual fight-or-flight mode, which was easily peaked. I didn't know it then, but I can see now that special education, as well-meaning as it was, had seeded a kind of PTSD in me that I have spent the last fifteen years grappling with. Given I'd seen my special education classmates put in closet-like holding rooms to get them to calm down (which only made them go more crazy), and put in restraints in front of me and other classmates, who wouldn't be upset by this? Once you've seen up close how cruel the well-meaning techniques of a behavioral plan are, you can't get them out of your head.

Every day became about calming me down at the end of the school day—patching me up, so to speak, and sending me back into the lion's den of special education the next morning.

My mom and dad had been working as animators with their own small animation studio. I remember all the wonderful colorful images on the computers. The focus of their jobs was to take someone's idea and make it happen. My mom was always saying, "Each project is its own unique puzzle." Realizing that school was only making my emotional state worse by the day, my parents decided I needed to be homeschooled. They shut the company down and my dad got a job in a corporation with benefits in order to help me out. Let me say that I understand now what a sacrifice this was for him. My dad had lived in India right after college and worked as a cameraman, following his guru around the world. Going corporate was a one-eighty pivot for him. My mom was one of those independent survivor types. She'd traveled all around the world on her own and was big on wilderness camping. She stopped working for money and I became the puzzle.

I was so anxious that I'd gotten to a state where I couldn't learn. So, my mom bought two of every book. She sat on one end of the couch and I sat on the other, facing each other. We worked on reading, doing it in tandem. I read a paragraph. Well, I struggled my way through reading a paragraph. She followed along and helped me with the pronunciation. Or, if there were a word I didn't know, we'd stop and look it up. Then, she would read a paragraph while I followed along, which helped me to learn prosody. She picked stories that had historical significance. One I remember, in particular, was called *My Brother Sam is Dead*, by James Lincoln Collier. It was about a boy and his brother during the Revolutionary War. I loved history. And, I loved the story.

Homeschooling was very healing. Not only did it give me a chance to calm down and find my own rhythm, but also my anxiety wasn't re-stimulated every day, keeping me in that state of hyper-vigilance that makes learning impossible. Part of what I did to recover was to steep myself in music and theater, which, as was evident in my childhood, was a kind of home base for me. Music led me back to myself. At first, I took a local community college drama class. The teacher, Mr. David, who was also the director, was very inclusive of all kinds of students. He didn't allow autism to be a problem for me, for him, or for the other classmates. I was who I was and that was good enough.

But, I was lucky; I could sing. I have perfect pitch and a nice singing voice. So, I got placed in some key situations in his musicals. The plays were hard work, but fun. I learned a lot about acting, singing, dancing, and moving in sync with others. Actors are playful and not as judgmental as classmates. It kind of back-doored a lot of relationship-based learning that I didn't get from the isolating experiences in special education. Also, because I was now at home with my mom all the time, it gave me a social group for a few hours a week.

When you are in a play, you become a temporary but cohesive group, working together for a common purpose—the fulfillment of the play. Because of my visual and auditory acuity and because, as a person with autism, I relished repetition, doing plays was an excellent venue for me. I knew not just my own cues and lines and positions, but also everyone else's as well. It was a kind of puzzle that I had worked out in my head. I even knew the lighting and sound cues.

This, in its own way, began to make math relevant. For example, at three minutes and forty seconds, I was to stand stage left by the first leg (side curtain on the stage, past the proscenium). I learned about dialogue and expression. In my mind's eye, I was back at Julia Morgan Theatre, from when I was two in the Cozy Room, only this time, I was on stage. I loved it.

Mr. David got angry sometimes. Unlike Cody, he was never punitive. His anger was surgical and, it seemed that no matter how upset he got, he was still able to show how much he truly cared to help the students be better actors and better people, making the play something everyone could enjoy and be proud to be part of. It was curious to me that I wasn't reacting to this teacher's anger as I would have expected, after being subjected to Cody's anger. I've thought about that for a long time. It seemed that Mr. David was clean with his anger. It was coming from a different place. He wasn't out to get anyone. It was powerful, but it wasn't a power trip. He used a loud voice to express that something needed to change. He just wanted to be heard. I got that. In a way, it was kind of a clean response to something not working. I found that I was able to trust him, because he expressed his anger so cleanly. Cody, on the other hand, seemed as if he was always ready to pounce. His under-the-surface anger didn't let up. It wasn't focused. It was ever-present, ready to burst. His emotional response felt lopsided and unfair. It didn't generate trust. It generated fear.

I'm not that little kid anymore and I've lived long enough to realize that life isn't necessarily fair. However, I've been thinking about how the power dynamics of special education impacted me. Kids with disabilities really struggle to do things that appear to be simple for other kids the same age. It doesn't help to be abused with words or overpowering actions, like holding a child down. What helps is calmness and being one-to-one with another person. This is what my mother offered. She didn't judge my reading. She just stopped at the stuck points and we hung out there together working on it from different angles until I got it. Then, we moved on to more words. She never punished me for what I didn't know or what I couldn't do. When I was finally able to articulate things that

I just didn't have words for, I began to build emotional depth into my own conversation. This is when all the stuff that had happened in special education came out. My parents felt sad. They said they suspected something was going on, but they didn't know exactly what it was and there weren't any bruises on my body to trigger alarm in their minds. Even I felt sad having to tell them. But, the PTSD has continued to dog me and it's been an apparent problem.

It took many points of entry to work on dealing with the impact of autism. But, little by little, my language has come together. My ability to read has flourished. After I started homeschool, I was lucky to have a really patient and creative math tutor who helped me through high school math. Her name was Sue Smith. She was so matter-of-fact. I know I made a lot of mistakes, but she somehow never made that a problem. It challenged her creativity as a teacher. She'd say, "Okay, Sam, let's try it this way." I still thought I was a math flunky. But, she shared with me that when she was in high school she thought she was bad at math, too. After high school, she found that she was good at math. So, she devoted her life to helping others who think they can't do math.

After high school, I had a somewhat parallel experience to Susan's. I took a math class in online college. It was such a great class that it turned me from a math-phobic into a math-lover. But, I still get triggered, in general, when I make mistakes at anything. It's the perception of having made a mistake that knuckles me under every time.

And yet, along the way, I have accomplished many wonderful things, including winning a director's award at the LA Film Festival for a short, coming-of-age student film. That was such a high! I received my award on the rooftop garden of the Hammer Museum in Los Angeles. Actor Jon Voigt was there, as well as Alice Braga. I got to have my pictures taken with them. It was all magical. I've written two books about life with autism. I've been writing for a magazine—*Autism File Magazine*—for four years, since the end of high school. After high school, I ran a film club for three and half years while studying bel canto singing with an excellent vocal teacher. I am a sought-after actor in my city. Most recently, I have been performing Puccini's "La Boheme" and Donizetti's "Daughter of the Regiment" with the San Francisco Pocket Opera. And, I have a sweet girlfriend. I've left Cody in the dust, baby!

Still, the PTSD from special education preschool dogs me every day. It's like a lightning bolt that jolts me when I least expect it. Going through autism, or any disability, is a heroic challenge and journey for the affected person and for his family. With your peers, it puts you on a different track, an out-of-sync track. In my case, I'm so lucky to have come this far. And I'm very relieved, grateful, and proud of that fact. But, that original stimulus is still in play within me. When the PTSD is stimulated, I'm suddenly back in that first special education class. The teachers are barking at me, making me sit cross-legged, slapping my face to make me talk, or making me miss being out in the sunshine, by demanding that I write lines on page. I can feel my hand hurting from holding a pencil. And I'm freaking out about ending up in the Lonely Chair. Or, if I make a mistake, I'm expecting Cody to come flying in like a freight train I never saw coming and run me over. So, I flip to hyper-vigilance before I even realize I'm there. It's automatic. I recognize it's like a trance. I am getting better at catching it, but it takes over before I realize what's going on.

Recently, I have found I love reading classical Greek tragedies. When these stories were written in the 5th century BCE, the Greek people were living in a state of perpetual PTSD, having endured eighty years of war and, at one point, having lost one third of their population to plague. One character, Ajax, has been instructive for me. He is a warrior. When his cousin Achilles is killed in battle, Ajax carries him and his armor off the battlefield. Because of this heroic deed, in his culture and in his time, Ajax would have been honored by being allowed to possess Achilles' armor. As a result, Ajax would ultimately be remembered as the guy who had earned the armor of Achilles, which would have bestowed dignity upon him and his family. This way of honoring was a form of conferring immortality on heroes back then. But, Agamemnon put him through a series of tests. Ajax did great on the first two, which had to do with his physical abilities. But on the third test, he had to use his words, and speech failed him. I related to this, of course. So, he lost the contest overall. The armor, which to him represented his self-worth and dignity, was taken away. As a result, he went mad, and ultimately killed himself.

Although this story was written over two thousand, five hundred years ago, it is a cautionary tale about the effects of PTSD even in our time. In Ajax's mind, when he failed the third part of the test, he failed everything. This is how PTSD works. There is a sense of overwhelming failure even in the face of great accomplishment. It snaps you into a kind of black and white thinking—all-or-nothing self-judgment.

How is it that the mind works this way? This is something I'm really curious about. Here I am at twenty-three, about to embark on the next great adventure of life and I am rendered into a hideous nervous wreck when I perceive I may be falling short in some way. It's not rational. Cody shows up in the strangest of places. Like Whack-a-Mole, he pops up and I have to push him down. On a feeling level, it's so real. At this point, I'm not a little kid, forced into the Lonely Chair in that first classroom or writing lines for that domineering teacher whose methodologies were so off. So, I have to ask myself, what power do I have? What is my part in this dance with my PTSD now?

I've gone over and over my options. There's walking away, medication, meditation, talk therapy, jogging, gym, boxing bag, consciously taking a breath. Still, Cody seems to be, literally, under my skin. In talking this over with my parents, we came to the idea of forgiveness. Can I really forgive Cody? For that matter, can I forgive that I ended up with autism?

A friend of mine recently said to me, "Sometimes your worse enemy is your best friend." In looking at the sources of my PTSD that way—special education and Cody, in particular—I think it's great that I'm aware of the cause of my distress. And I can see there is a pattern of cause and effect. I can see also that this pattern ignites a specific belief I have about myself that was formed back then, and that I have been carrying that belief forward in present time without updating it to the present circumstances. The belief is this: It's just not okay to make mistakes.

I am reminded of a time in first grade where this bully, Jackson, who was also my classmate, kept coming after me. I was a goofy-looking, non-athletic kid with glasses. Whenever we were near the part of the playground that had rocks, Jackson would figure out how to trip me. I ended up going to the ER twice at the hands of Jackson. But, curiously, I don't have "Jackson PTSD." A few years later, I ran into him at a local grocery store. I said, "Hey, Jackson, you owe me an apology for kicking my ass in first grade." He said, "Oh, I forgot. I'm sorry." My after-school teacher saw the interaction and jumped in to solidify the interchange of forgiveness by suggesting that we shake on it, which we did. I accepted Jackson's apology and that somehow completed it for me. I did know about Jackson in first grade—that he was the first kid to be dropped off at school, at about 6:30 a.m., in his pajamas, with a shopping bag with his clothes and cereal in it. He was the last kid to be picked up at the end of the day, after all the other kids had left, except for our first grade teacher, who waited for one of his parents to pick him up. Knowing this about him later in life gave me compassion for him. Even then, I recognized that Jackson was doing the best he could. So, it was easy to forgive him when the opportunity presented itself.

In thinking about this, I realize that compassion, humility, and forgiveness need to figure into my updated analysis of Cody. I really don't know anything about his personal life. What was going on in his world? Thinking about it like this, I can forgive Cody. He, too, was doing the best he could. I have to believe this and I do on most days. His belief system included acting like a strict father and implementing the behavioral intervention techniques he learned. I don't think this means I have to understand him. But, now that I'm over a decade away from that guy, I can release my grudge against him. I know just because I said so doesn't mean I've waived a magic wand and made the feeling go away for good. Perhaps, a more practical strategy would be when I feel the Cody Effect coming on, I can let Nigel over-dub it with Vivaldi's "Four Seasons" and set the world right once again.

The Hearing Child

Kevin Souhrada

I am a second-generation deaf man, from a predominantly deaf family. My parents and my two younger sisters are deaf. My mother is the only deaf member in her entire family, and very possibly the first deaf person in her family lineage. But my paternal grandparents, who are hearing, were not surprised when they discovered my father was deaf, because I have a lot of deaf relatives on my father's side. Even to this day, I am still discovering more people that are related to me who are deaf, just like me.

I was born in Mitchell, South Dakota, in a hospital about five blocks from the world famous Corn Palace, which is now a county jail. I spent my elementary years in Edgerton, Minnesota, a small farming town located in the southwestern corner of the state. My life consisted of going on hour and a half round trips from Edgerton to Sioux Falls, South Dakota, on Fridays and Saturdays, to get my deaf social fix at the South Dakota Association of the Deaf Recreational Center, a place where deaf people gather together to drink, to share news, to watch captioned films on loan from the National Captioning Institute (this was during a time when only two to three TV programs and shows per night were captioned), to hold meetings for their respective organizations, to hold fundraising events, and to just be themselves after a hard week of working and functioning in a world that was, and still is, designed to work for hearing people.

Naturally, my first language was American Sign Language (ASL). I remember being able to carry on a conversation with deaf adults, but I also remember being confused with English rules and ASL rules, as they are vastly different. For instance, ASL is not a written language, but it has been proven to be a true language with its own grammar rules and syntax. Whenever we read books, watched TV, or drove around, my parents would teach me ASL and English vocabulary.

Just like every other deaf person living in a world designed for hearing people, we required adaptive devices, such as captioning machines and flashing lights for the telephone and doorbell. My parents also required flashing lights for us when we were babies, so they'd know if we were crying or not. We "talked" on the phone via a huge machine called a teletypewriter, or, as we called it, The Green Monster. It was indeed a monster, with its sheer size and weight. It looked like one of those machines you'd find in a printing shop. It was about four feet wide and two feet deep. It sent a light vibration throughout our mobile home every time it printed on a roll of paper. The roll of paper was yellow with green lines; the same kind you find on office notepads. The keyboard was hard for kids to use, as well as older people who suffered from arthritis. We were able to communicate with other deaf people who had The Green Monster, by taking the headset of a phone and putting it on an adapter that looks like the main body of a phone, but without buttons, and is wired to the machine. At fourteen years old, I learned The Green Machine was immensely heavy when I helped my father and his friend carry one from the ground level of our house to the basement. We had to use two by fours to slide it down the stairs, because we couldn't lift it.

For fourteen years, I lived in a fourteen by seventy foot trailer house, with three bedrooms and one bathroom. It housed seven of us: my parents, my two sisters, my foster brother, my foster sister, and me. The house was crowded, but I had a happy childhood in that house. In many ways, that house was perfect for deaf people. For instance, if you pounded your foot on the floor, the vibration reverberated throughout the house, making it easier to get our attention. The same was true for the walls. Suppertime at the house was vibrant and lively. We all could have several conversations going at the same time—a skill that is usually learned by deaf people in deaf families, or at residential schools for the deaf.

I remember the day we first got a closed captioning machine from Sears. My father hooked it up to the TV and we'd reserve our nights at certain times for the captioned programs. We called it family time. We'd have deaf friends over on weeknights, since the Deaf Center was only open on weekends. Our house was like the Deaf Center, but on a much smaller scale.

Like every other deaf person, I was left with no choice but to interact with hearing people on a daily basis, people who were different from me even though we were all Americans. When I was a kid, I was usually the only deaf student at the public schools I attended. I started my education at a public school in a small town and most of the interpreters I had signed Signed Exact English (SEE), which consisted of signing every word, such as "butter" and "fly" in butterfly, whereas my first language was American Sign Language (ASL). ASL is the only natural sign language used by deaf people in this country, and it is typically offered as one of the foreign language options in schools and colleges.

Imagine a bunch of kids sitting in a classroom, and me walking in with a short, seventies haircut, plaid pants, a button shirt, a pair of cowboy boots, a body hearing aid, and two wires leading to ear molds in both ears. Yep, I got quite a few stares and some not so nice stares.

Before I entered the fifth grade, we relocated back to South Dakota after my father got laid off—even though he was one of the hardest and longest tenured workers at his company. (We all suspected his being deaf was the sole reason for the lay off.) I continued my education at public schools in several towns as a full-time student. I enrolled at the now closed South Dakota School for the Deaf (SDSD) before my sophomore year, and was dual enrolled at a local public school. Then, I was fully enrolled at SDSD during my senior year. When I graduated, I became a second generation SDSD alumnus, since my parents graduated from the same school. I have several deaf relatives who graduated from SDSD as well. In fact, my father's family history is so engrained in SDSD's legacy that almost every one of us had the same literature teacher, who taught there for forty-two years.

When my graduation was approaching, since I was class president, I was supposed to give a speech. I wrote my speech and gave it to my class advisor so she could go over it. One glance and she gave it back to me and said, "I don't know why I asked you to give your speech to me. I usually end up correcting the students' English and I never have to with yours." English is my second language and I have been told I have better command of the language than many hearing people. I have since found my passion for writing poems, and have written over four hundred and forty poems to date. I hope to have them published one day.

I have two younger sisters that are technically "hard of hearing," which means they are able to hear and talk via telephone with the assistance of hearing aids. Their educational experience was vastly different from mine. My younger sister was mainstreamed all her life except for one year at SDSD, whereas my youngest sister spent her first three elementary years at SDSD, and then spent the rest at a public school where she became the head cheerleader. They had no problem making friends and almost no one picked on them. I was envious of them, as well as resentful, but eventually I got over it. While they were at SDSD, the teachers and the administration team kept telling them it was not the proper placement for them at SDSD, and, like me, they were too advanced.

As I mentioned, my parents are also deaf. My father spent his entire life at SDSD, while my mother started at a small, one-room farm school in the middle of nowhere near Winner, SD. Her gradual hearing decline reached the point where she had trouble understanding the teacher, so her parents decided to have her transferred to SDSD when she was in the fourth grade. My parents' time at SDSD was so different from my time there. Back then, the campus was located outside of the city, and had a farm. The boys would get up in the morning and do farm chores before heading to school. The girls were responsible for cooking meals and cleaning the kitchen. After school, the boys headed back to the farm to work some more, and then back to the dormitory for study hall and bedtime. The girls, again, cooked meals and cleaned the kitchen, and then it was study hall and bedtime for them as well.

After graduation, my mother went to Gallaudet University, the world's only liberal arts college for the deaf in Washington, D.C. She attended for two years, and then had to leave due to the riots taking place there after the assassination of Dr. Martin Luther King Jr. My father never went to college. They tested his hearing for admissions to Gallaudet University, but the result was that his hearing was too high for him to be eligible, even though the nerves leading from his ears to the brain never developed. He held a few jobs over the years, such as printing (it was a popular occupation for deaf men during his time) and maintenance.

During my years as a mainstreamed deaf student, I was the first deaf student at every public school I attended, the first deaf student to participate in 4-H in southern Minnesota (including contests where I got blue ribbons in drawing and woodworking), the first deaf kid to play t-ball for the local team, the first deaf student to make it to the top three in the forty meter dash, the first deaf student to play fifth grade basketball, the first deaf student to play middle school football, the first deaf student to take Spanish class in the history of the Sioux Falls Public School District, and I was one of two deaf students taking the national Spanish exam in the entire nation (a first for the organization who provided the exams).

My quest to take Spanish class started when I was registering for classes. I read that in order to graduate, a student needs to take up a foreign language class. I chose Spanish and turned in my paperwork. The next day, they informed me I could not take the Spanish class. When I asked why, they told me since I could not hear and speak, I could not learn Spanish. I shot back, "But I can learn how to read and write in Spanish. You're not going to tell me I can't take Spanish class, then tell me I can't graduate just because I don't have any foreign language credit." That went back and forth for a week and the principal got involved. The superintendent almost got involved, but finally they gave in.

They had to make some modifications to how they taught the class, which included slowing down a little so my interpreter had time to catch up. (My interpreter was also learning Spanish at the same time.) The class also consisted of a lot of listening to audiotapes. The school hired someone to type every single word on all the audiotapes, so every time the students listened to an audiotape, my teacher could give me a copy of the transcript to read along. I had one of the highest grades in that class.

In fifth grade, I was a 4.0 GPA honor roll student—the first deaf student in that school's history to achieve that. Another first, eh? The kids would make fun of me and call me deaf and dumb. So many times during class, we'd get our tests back and the kids would ask me for my grade. I'd show them the paper, which usually had a big red "A" on it. I'd ask them to show theirs and they'd refuse. I'd tease them, "What's wrong? You just realized you're dumber than I am?" Oh, how they hated it when I did that.

One year, the school decided to put me in the Future Problem Solvers club. It was short-lived because the kids refused to talk to me and kept telling me I was in the wrong place. The teacher who was responsible for the club was of no help. So one day, during one of the club activities, I walked out. Maybe it was not the best way of dealing with it, but yeah, I just had enough.

During our P.E. class, one of my favorite games to play was dodgeball. I'd keep a mental list of the kids who picked on me during that day and purposely throw the ball at their heads. The rule was: once we aim for the head, we're out. I was fine with that, because the satisfaction that came after the ball hit their head was too damn great to refuse. Hey, don't call me mean, because I know a lot of people out there would agree with me on this one – possibly including you!

During those public school years, I was unhappy, frustrated, and angry. All that went away when I went to summer camps. For five summers in a row, my parents sent me to three different camps: Summer Program for the Gifted Hearing Impaired Students (BTC), in Boys Town, Nebraska; Camp Mark Seven (CM7), in Old Forge, New York; and Youth

Leadership Camp (YLC), in Stayton, Oregon. The camps were for deaf students under the age of eighteen. Deaf like me. I was at my happiest at those three camps.

All the girlfriends I had were from those summer camps. My first make-out session happened when I was thirteen years old. The girl was fourteen, from Arkansas, and *she was cute*! I'm telling you: *c-u-t-e*! She had blue eyes, bangs and dirty blonde, shoulder-length hair. Her perfume had this distinctive smell and, even to this day, I think of her every time I smell that particular perfume, which seldom happens. Unfortunately, our make-out session lasted for maybe ten seconds. We made out in a corner on the sofa, and the corner faces the hallway where people, including camp counselors, walk. Well, I stopped, because I had a feeling one of the counselors was going to come up to us. Sure enough, right after we stopped, one of the lead counselors came up and asked what we were up to. I told him, "Oh, we were chatting about boyfriends and girlfriends." Close call, but yeah, I think the fact that it lasted for only ten seconds still pisses me off to this day.

At YLC, I met my first love. She was deaf and beautiful. She was perfect in every way. She had long brown locks and smooth tan skin. One thing I loved the most about her was the way she'd walk away from me, with her head turned to face me, smirking. Oh, that smirk! She was mainstreamed and her social life was lively, unlike mine. She wasn't the first deaf student at her school and the school, staff, and students knew about ASL and deaf culture. I told her she was lucky. My school was exactly the opposite. I lived in South Dakota and she lived in Virginia. We dated for a year and a half, but the long distance drove a wedge in our relationship.

When I look back, I find it interesting there were clashes between us based on our beliefs in terms of us being deaf.

She came from a hearing family and I didn't. She didn't understand why I had to go to the Deaf Center every Friday and Saturday night to get my social fix, whereas she'd go out with her deaf and hearing friends almost every night.

I have held jobs that enabled me the unique opportunity to work with the deaf community, such as Sound Mental Health, in Seattle, Washington, where I worked as a case manager working with deaf clients. I also volunteered my time as a member and officer of several deaf organizations, such as South Dakota Association of the Deaf (SDAD) and Greater Seattle Club of the Deaf (GSCD). I have also served as a parent representative and president of the Rocky Mountain Deaf School, in Golden, Colorado.

My parents were also longtime members and officers of several deaf organizations, such as National Fraternal Society of the Deaf and International Catholic Deaf Association. My mother was the longest serving president of SDAD. My sisters now hold paid positions in which they ensure deaf and hard of hearing children of South Dakota are getting fair options, such as school placement, communication mode, and the like.

All this information is critical for you, the reader, to understand why I'm choosing to share my experience of having hearing children with you. It's something that a significant number of deaf people experience. It is estimated that about ninety percent of deaf adults have hearing children. We call them CODAs (Children of Deaf Adults). The ten percent of deaf adults who have deaf children are looked upon as lucky. The idea of a deaf adult from a deaf family having a hearing child is usually considered strange, and, for some, a disappointment. It is pretty much the same as a hearing couple finding out their child is deaf. However, that does not mean they (the hearing parents) and we (the deaf parents) love our children any less. This unique kind of parent-child situation is something that's often discussed within the deaf community, but not often enough that the general population is aware of it. So, I chose to share my story in hopes of reaching out to more people, so they'll have a better understanding of deaf people in my situation.

***

I first became a father at the age of twenty-four. The woman I was dating gave birth to a healthy baby girl. It was time for her hearing test and upon finding out she was deaf, her mother, who was also deaf, was not happy. She did not want our daughter to endure the hardships that we'd endured. But when I found out, I jumped for joy! Oh, I was happy! My child was like me! She was perfect! Usually, hearing parents have an entirely different reaction when they find out their child is deaf, and I think it is based on how the message is delivered by the doctor, which usually goes like this, "I'm sorry, but your baby has a degree of hearing loss and he/she will have a very hard life ahead of him/her." But for me, a deaf adult, this was the best news.

She's one of the members of the next generation that will ensure that our deaf community, language, and traditions will continue. She is also the third generation in my family who is deaf. She learned the same language and the same traditions as I did, she faced barriers and struggles just like I did, she achieved her goals just like I did, and she participated in the deaf community, just like I did. She went to a public school that had a deaf program, which had about forty elementary deaf and hard of hearing students. They did not put an emphasis on being a deaf person, American Sign Language, or, most importantly, education. After three years of fighting, I decided to relocate to Colorado and enrolled her at the Rocky Mountain

Deaf School, a bilingual (ASL and English) and bicultural school that is run by an almost entirely deaf staff. She thrived as a deaf person and I was so elated to see that.

Fast forward to the year 2012. I was already married for a year to a wonderful woman. She is gentle and patient with me, and my antics. (I am the kind of person that would rather do something stupid than do nothing at all, and say something stupid rather than say nothing at all.) In September of that year, we welcomed a baby boy to this world. He was perfect. During the pregnancy, my wife, who is also deaf, and I argued about whether the baby was deaf or not. I was so sure my deaf genes would prevail, as it did with my oldest daughter.

We, along with my mother-in-law, walked with the nurse, baby in hand, into the room where the hearing test was to be conducted. It had a little plastic box where the baby was to be placed and hooked up to a monitor. The nurse attached my precious son with two wires suctioned on his head—one right on the forehead and the second one just above his left ear. We, with bated breath, watched the monitor do its thing. The word "pass" came up on the screen. For those who do not know, if a baby "passes" the hearing test, then the baby is hearing, while "fail" is the word that comes up when the baby is deaf. Fail and being deaf is not a very good combination of words, as it already sets the tone that being deaf is a bad thing.

So anyways, when I saw the word "pass," my world, the world as I knew it, the deaf world that I've always lived in, the deaf world that defined who I was, am, and will be, all came crashing down like a meteor striking a utopian paradise. The nurse looked at us, smiled, and said the baby is doing well. My mother-in-law stood there with a smile on her face (my mother-in-law thinks all deaf people should get cochlear implants—a taboo subject of ours). Oh, how badly I wanted to erase that damn smile off her face. It was the smile that every parent has when they find out their child is "perfect," meaning he/she is not deaf.

I stood there in shock and soon that shock turned into anger and disappointment. But, he was my son. My son. Mine. My blood. The one who will carry my precious last name into the next generation. I loved him, and still love him, all the same. As my son lay in the plastic crib with the hospital logo, I looked at him and said, "You will change the world, starting with my family-in-law. You will be one of the best CODAs (Child of Deaf Adult)."

Cochlear implants. This is an issue that sharply divides the deaf community and the medical community. Unfortunately, that is not the only thing that is being divided. I have seen the mere mention of cochlear implants cause rifts within the deaf community. I have seen this happen within families as well. It is a sensitive topic that we, as a deaf community, have yet to come to a consensus on, in my opinion. A cochlear implant is a device that has four parts: a sound processor that is worn behind the ear or the body, which captures sound and processes it into digital code; a coil, which is connected to the processor and attaches itself to a magnet that's inserted underneath your skin right above the ear; a magnet, which is connected to an implant that enters your ear through the skull; and the implant itself, which has electrodes that simulate the cochlea's hearing nerve, which then sends impulses to the brain, and then the brain interprets the impulses as sounds.

Doctors and audiologists alike think it is the greatest invention for deaf people. They will try to "encourage" you to have your child implanted without telling you about hearing aids. Why? The total cost of one cochlear implant, along with surgery, device, and rehabilitation, can cost as much as $100,000, and is covered by most insurance companies. Hearing aids, however, are either fully or partially covered by *some* insurance companies and are not covered by Medicaid. Granted, there are some deaf people who feel they function better with cochlear implants. I do not agree with this, but I do support people's choices.

What I am opposed to is cochlear implants being put in babies as young as six months old. Those babies had no choice! Often enough, parents are left with the false impression their implanted babies will grow up to be "hearing." Yes, I admit, there are *some* success stories out there. *Some*. Not many. The majority of deaf people that get implants throw them away as they get older. As for the educational aspect for deaf people with cochlear implants, they usually have speech therapy included in their Individualized Education Program (IEP), where they spend maybe an hour, maybe three hours a day, practicing their speech. Often the schools are so focused on that part, they neglect the rest of the child's education. As a result, they fall behind, and when the schools realize their approach isn't working, they "dump" the students at either a state school for the deaf or a deaf program, and then the burden of getting that student up to par falls on them. My wife was one of the first people to get a cochlear implant, but it did not work and she had the implants removed.

We thought—we honestly thought—the reactions we got from the nurses and my mother-in-law, after finding out our son was hearing, was reserved for a hospital setting. After all, people working in hospitals are typically focused on treating everything like a disease. But, little did we realize, those reactions were just the first of many.

We got home from the hospital exhausted, and once we got our energy and mojo back, we went to work making adjustments around the house. The first thing we did was turn up the volume on the TV—something we never needed to do— for our son. Once he reached the point where he was starting to develop language, he learned ASL first, and then English. It got to the point where he'd switch languages in the same sentence—something that I, personally, wasn't used to. Once he got a grasp of the English language, he'd choose to speak English rather than sign ASL, which, at first, irritated me, but not my wife, because she was used to it with her hearing family. He'd start conversations with random strangers, and I kept reminding him to be careful. He continues to do so to this day, to my dismay, but other deaf parents I've spoken with say their own kids do the same thing.

When it was time for Sage to start going to school, we chose a Montessori school, because we really liked the approach and philosophy. I was excited for him, but my excitement turned to disappointment when I realized we were the only deaf parents in the entire school. Our good friends, whose son went to the same school, knew ASL, and that helped a little. We soon relocated to Washington State and enrolled him in another Montessori school. This was an entirely different experience, as we were the only deaf family, and the only family that used ASL. My communication with the hearing parents consisted of "Hi" and more "Hi." The language barrier was frustrating me. I remember sitting down with my wife and saying, "You mean to tell me I have to go through this for the next eighteen freaking years, trying to communicate with hearing parents!?!"

We started to notice his teacher and the other parents would talk on a daily basis when they came to pick their kids up after school. That is how the other parents knew what was going on with their kids. When it came to my wife and me, we'd just go in, say "Hi" to the teacher, and get our son. We knew very little about what was going on, so the idea of a parent-teacher conference came up. We requested an ASL interpreter. We had a good discussion and we expressed our desire to know more about our son. It wasn't until then that his teacher realized why we knew so little, so we started to receive updates via a weekly email describing his weekly activities, progress, and struggles. (Another small solution to an everyday communication barrier.) Oh, and we were the first deaf parents to send their child to both schools. Another first, eh?

One day, the director of the school asked parents to volunteer at the school. I was one of the volunteers and when I showed up, the mother who was responsible for the whole thing pointed to a pile of rocks, mulch, and gravel, and then pointed to the wheelbarrow. Yup, okay, so I shoveled and shoveled. At some point, I grew tired of shoveling, so I joined in on another volunteer project that involved woodworking. Woodworking was my passion. I showed the other parents what I was capable of doing, and the mother in charge gave me a surprised look, said "good job," and then walked away.

The end of the school year carnival was fun—for my son. We just walked around chatting with each other. Some of the other parents looked at us and whispered to each other. That was okay—we were used to it. But it does not mean we like it. Every deaf person I know is used to it.

Now, my son shows almost complete fluency in both English and ASL, but the language of his choice is always English. He signs with us, and then naturally changes to spoken English. We have to keep reminding him we are deaf. He knows to tap us on the shoulder to get our attention, and he informs us when something is making noise. He tells his friends his parents are deaf. (He also tells people his dad fixes everything and his mom can't fix anything.)

Then, what I thought was a first and last time happened— my wife got pregnant again. She wanted a girl. Naturally, I wanted another boy. She asked me if I thought the baby would be deaf or hearing. I said I was not going down that road again. The day came and she had a fast birth. We went through the same routine, walking to the room where the hearing test was to be conducted. My third and final child was declared hearing. I was surprised and my surprise, once again, turned to disappointment, but it was easier for me to accept the second time around.

It is common knowledge that girls develop faster than boys, as well as younger siblings, when they're learning from their older siblings. Our daughter seems to have the deaf DNA built in—more than what my son has. She is not yet two and already knows to tap on my leg and then point to the door when someone comes and knocks on the door. She is picking up ASL faster than her brother. She is also very expressive and facial expressions are one of the main parts of ASL.

I am now a forty-four-year-old deaf man with long hair and a beard. Since I am only five foot four inches tall, sometimes I am called "The Little Bigfoot." I have three beautiful children. My oldest deaf daughter is now twenty, my hearing son is now five, and my youngest hearing daughter is now twenty-one months old.

My wife has more patience dealing with hearing people than I do. If the time comes to deal with hearing people, I will do it with no problem, but if my wife is with me, I send her to deal with it. She's fine with it, because she knows she's nicer about it than I am. Having hearing children has taught me a lot. I think the most valuable lesson I could ever learn was unconditional love. Yes, my hearing children are different than I am, but at the same time, we're not so different at all. I just wish the world would see us that way, not as something they can make money off of, not as something that is not important, not something, but somebody. Our communication differences do come up once in a while and I do get frustrated, but hey, my children have every right to be with people who are like them, just as I have the right to be around people like me.

Ask any deaf person, blind person, wheelchair user, anyone with superpowers, and they will tell you the exact same damn thing. The system, set forth by our government, looks at us as a group of broken people that cost too much money and too much work (closed captions, interpreters, signs in Braille, wheelchair ramps, and so much more). We do not see ourselves that way. We see ourselves simply as a group of people that wants to exist and to live our lives the same way everyone else does. That is why I am depending on my children to make a difference in this world, not just for themselves, but also for everyone from all walks of life. No more firsts, everyone's on the same level. Not above, not below, the exact same level.

By now, I have to admit, I'm starting to get tired of being first: first this, first that, and first everywhere. And I am not the only one who feels that way. For once, I'd like to be on the same level as the majority of the population. I'm nobody special, I am one of you, and you are one of us. I just happen to be deaf, and yes, I am proud of it.

I Did It

Cathy Beaudoin

"**D**ave, things aren't good," I cried into the phone.

"Whadaya mean 'things aren't good'?"

"I got a D on my first stats exam, and now they think I'm dumb," I replied.

Six weeks into the accounting PhD program at Drexel University, I had gotten a D on my first statistics exam. *Oh crap*, I thought to myself. *I can't fake this anymore.* My problem with statistics was simple. I could not see the blackboard, and had never told anyone at school I was legally blind. After about five seconds, I felt the need to defend myself to Dave.

"You know I just can't see the board, right?"

Then, in a moment of horror, the fact that my worst grade in the MBA program at Columbia University had been in statistics flashed through my head. I had to remind myself I still had passed the class.

"I mean, I thought I knew what was going on. I figured I knew enough to pass the first exam." My face burned with embarrassment. "I was doing okay on the homework."

A sense of panic overwhelmed me. If I didn't get my doctorate, I had no other plan. I heard Dave pound his foot on the floor and groan, his typical reaction to being presented with a new problem to solve.

"You got a D, huh. That's not like you." Always one to be brutally honest, he laughed and added, "But then again, statistics isn't exactly playing to your strength, either."

"Hey, that's not nice. I'm going to flunk out of the program. One F and I'm out."

"Oh, come on now. That's not going to happen." And with those words, Dave offered to tutor me. While I had called Dave hoping to get some advice, I wasn't expecting such a simple solution. I should have known better. Long before losing my eyesight, I had worked for Dave at MetLife in Manhattan. He was an actuary, the smartest guy I ever met, and one of the few men I knew who did everything he could to help women advance up through the management ranks.

"How you gonna do that?" I asked.

"Over the phone."

"Great, I'm blind, and you're gonna teach me stats over the phone. That sounds like fun."

"That's exactly what I'm gonna do. But I'm tellin' you now, you have to do exactly what I say. You're gonna work harder than you've ever worked before. And if you can't take the criticism, then it won't work. I don't care if you can't see anymore. If I'm going to tutor you, you just need to listen to me."

I knew Dave was going to be hard on me. But I also knew if I did exactly what he told me to do, I'd learn the material and pass the class. And, as an added bonus, I had an excuse to talk to one of my friends on a regular basis. This brought me great comfort, since I was living in a new city, and lonely.

"Not a problem," I said. After all, one of my core competencies was my willingness to work hard.

The documents certifying my blindness had been signed more than six months before the fall semester started. But, when school started, I still wasn't ready to identify myself as a person with a disability. In fact, for the first six weeks of the semester, I'd used my white cane to walk to school, and then hidden it in my backpack once I entered the business school building. Getting a D on the statistics exam forced me to face my biggest fear: if I revealed my secret, others would judge me as less capable.

When I realized I wasn't going to be able to continue my career as an accountant, I decided to apply to doctoral programs in accounting. Teaching was something I always wanted to do, and I loved my profession, so combining the two seemed the perfect solution. Initially, I was more worried about not being a viable PhD candidate, because I was older, in my early forties. Luckily, the age factor was obscured, at least on paper, by the fact that I didn't get my undergraduate degree in accounting until the age of twenty-seven. Once people started calling me for on-campus interviews, I decided not to tell anyone about my blindness until after I was accepted into a program. I wanted to make sure people knew I was smart and determined *before* they found out I was blind. Luckily, I had enough peripheral vision to navigate without walking into walls or people, and reading was never part of the interview process. Though I didn't believe I was less qualified than anyone else applying, I was worried the faculty evaluating candidates might discriminate against me, even if only subconsciously.

My concern about getting accepted into a doctoral program had its merit. When I applied to PhD programs, there were only about sixty-five schools in the United States that offered a PhD in accounting. Most schools accepted only two or three students a year, and the dropout rate from these programs was around fifty percent. So it was neither easy to get into a program, nor was graduation a given. Ultimately, my strategy for handling the interview process was effective. I was accepted at four schools. Since I had lived in Manhattan for the past eight years, my preference was to stay as close to the city as possible. I chose to enroll at Drexel University in Philadelphia.

Getting a D on that first exam was a huge red flag. I hemmed and hawed for a half a day, seriously considered ignoring the problem the grade signaled, and then came to my senses and made an appointment with the coordinator for the business school doctoral program.

"Dr. G., I just wanted to meet with you because I found out I got a D on my first stat exam."

He did not respond. Because the walls in the conference room where we met were white, I could make out the outline of his body. But the details were elusive, blurred beyond recognition. Did he have brown or black hair? Did he wear glasses? Were his arms crossed? I pointed my eyes at him, but could not see the expression on his face.

"Um... It's not what you think. Um... The real problem is, um, the real problem is that I can't see the board."

Dr. G maintained his silence. I felt like I was going to vomit.

"I mean, I'm legally blind. I just never told anybody."

This time I waited for a response and, after what seemed like the longest minute of my life, it finally came. "How do you know it's not an aptitude problem?"

"An aptitude problem?" I laughed out loud. "Seriously?"

My instincts kicked in. "I was a Vice President of Finance in a large, publicly traded company, and have a degree from Columbia University. I'm pretty sure it's not an aptitude problem."

I let the words sink in.

"I just wanted to make sure you knew this one grade wasn't indicative of my future performance in the program," I continued. "I'm going to have to figure out how to make this work given I can't see the board. I'm doing fine in all my other classes. But they don't require the same kind of visual precision when I'm trying to learn something new."

"I guess we'll see about that, won't we?"

At those words I got up and left. Needing to go have the same conversation with the head of the Accounting PhD program, I steeled myself for the same response. Of course they're going to be pissed. They'll think they wasted a slot on me. And while I'm sure the head of the accounting program was concerned when I told him about my secret, he kept any doubts about my ability to be successful to himself. I think he was much more sensitive to the implications around the Americans with Disabilities Act. After all, I was in the program, and had no plans to leave it.

Though I finally told people at Drexel about my disability, I felt like the problem of being blind and succeeding in the PhD program was mine to solve. It never occurred to me to ask about any special assistance or accommodation. It was not my way. I learned early in life, when my mother unexpectedly passed away, and my father could not cope, it was up to me to take care of myself. After watching my father fall apart, I vowed to be strong no matter what happened to me.

When I decided to try to get my doctorate, there were no blind people in the United States getting PhDs in any of the business disciplines, at least not that I knew of. And I definitely didn't know of any other blind students getting a PhD in accounting. Desperate to know others had done what I was trying to do, I spent many nights searching the Internet for blind business school professors. There were a few professors in areas like psychology or sociology, but none teaching in disciplines where visual precision mattered in the classroom. Unsuccessful in my quest, I found comfort in knowing I had a set of skills from my seventeen-year career in both public accounting and industry to fall back on, and was hopeful I could leverage my work experience in an academic setting. In the end, it was my network of friends, most of whom I worked with in some capacity in a business setting, that helped me adapt to my situation, and provided a helping hand when things started to feel unmanageable.

As soon as Dave offered to tutor me, he bought my textbook and I bought a digital recorder. I taped my stats class, and sent him the file via email. He listened to the class after he got home from work, and then we talked at night. With me standing at my kitchen counter, my ear burning from the phone being pressed against it for hours at a time, Dave explained the material in excruciating detail. We did extra problems together, and we laughed a lot. But when I was alone at night, I agonized over the thought of failing. It never happened. Because of Dave's generosity, I got a B in that stat course, and an A in the next one. I guess it wasn't an aptitude problem after all. And regardless of what others thought, I knew I was capable.

Learning statistics was not the only problem I had that fall. Figuring out how to function as a blind person in an academic setting was another issue altogether. Essentially, I had no central vision in my left eye, and very blurry vision in my right eye. If you put a dollar bill directly in front of me, I couldn't see it. But if there were a quarter on the ground between my feet, I'd see it clearly because of my peripheral vision. One way to work with this type of limited vision is to use low-vision tools. Just before school started, I experimented with several of these devices. My assumption was I'd find the one that helped the most, and get comfortable using it. Initially, I tried a set of hand-held magnifiers. Then, I tried a couple of electronic devices that enlarged the typical twelve-point font used on a printed page to twenty-four- or thirty-six-point font for any text passed under the reader.

I never got comfortable with any of the tools I tried. The magnifiers were fine if I needed to read a label on a can, but not as useful when trying to read, and comprehend, the volume of material required of a doctoral student. Magnifying text certainly made it easier to see words on a page, but reading is not simply a matter of seeing a word; it is understanding where the word is positioned in a sentence, or where a sentence is positioned within a paragraph. Maintaining a death grip on my old ways, swapping larger font size for less information about where a word fell on a page was a tradeoff I was still unwilling to make. Instead, I preferred to press my left eye right up against a page, or a computer screen, and read with the limited amount of vision I had.

During my first year of doctoral studies, it was my friends, Anne and John, who, when visiting, saw how much I was struggling with my low vision. Anne and John were married, my age, and, though we didn't meet until we were adults, grew up in the same suburb in Northern Connecticut as I did. Anne was a successful real estate agent, and John was the chief operating officer at a small engineering company. Both were hands-on problem solvers. Without hesitation, they stepped in to help where they could. They started with the simple things, like optimizing my computer setup. With their help, I purchased my first twenty-seven-inch monitor. Then, John modified the accessibility settings on my computer. The fonts on the desktop were enlarged to one hundred and ninety percent of their normal size, and the icons were adjusted to look three times as large as the default setting. Finally, the various toolbars and other settings within the applications for spreadsheets and word documents were enlarged. Changing the settings was much easier than adjusting to the way everything looked on my computer screen. For months thereafter, every time I sat down to do my schoolwork, I was forced to face the reality of my blindness.

Anne and John also helped me install software that read text out loud. Again, I had trouble adjusting to the software, because it required a change in how I worked. Listening and learning was a much different mental process than reading and learning. I was used to reading a paragraph, pausing to absorb the material, thinking about the material, and then moving on to the next paragraph. I found it difficult to create the space in my brain to absorb new information when my mental energy was focused on listening. It felt like I was wired to learn with my eyes, not my ears.

Frustrated by my inability to adapt, I went online and bought more magnifiers, searching for the one that would bring my vision back. Of course, it didn't happen, and still unwilling to yield, I simply continued to read my textbooks by putting my left eye up against the printed page, and tilting my head to the right. The unnatural posture put a strain on my eyes and neck, and caused constant headaches. Despite the physical discomfort, it just seemed easier to accept reading as a slow and painful process. I slogged forward as best as I could, head down, no distractions.

As frustrated as I was with trying to adapt to my blindness, I found comfort in being able to walk the streets and neighborhoods in downtown Philadelphia. I lived in the Center City area, and one of the jewels of the city, Rittenhouse Square, was only a five-minute walk from my apartment. I'd often find myself sitting on a bench in the park, watching the outlines of bodies passing by me, and listening to people's conversations. I'd imagine what their lives were like, and the stress from trying to rebuild my career usually eased up. On the weekends, I'd walk along the bike path that paralleled the Schuylkill River. Unless it was the dead of winter, there were usually rowers on the river, and lots of runners and bikers passing by on the path. Sunday mornings were often reserved for longer walks in the city. One of my favorites was to head to South Street, about a two-mile walk, where all the hipster bars and restaurants are. Though it often smelled like an open dumpster, I had many fond memories of this area. When my friends from central New Jersey came to visit, we'd often sit outside on some patio, have cocktails and share stories about life. Once I made it to South Street, I'd head north for about fifteen blocks, and then west back to my place. The entire loop took me about two hours to walk, and I always felt happy and re-energized when I got back home. Then I'd settle back into my school routine, either spending the rest of the day doing homework, or research, or both.

Getting outside on a regular basis was important since passing the stats course and trying to figure out how to work with my low vision were not the only hurdles I faced in the PhD program. Unlike most other doctoral programs, the business school at Drexel required students to take two comprehensive exams, one at the end of the first year of classes, and one at the end of the second year. The first year exam covered the two statistics courses, microeconomics, macroeconomics, two finance courses, and a basic research methodology course taught by Dr. G. I took some psychology courses that year, too, but they were not on the first comprehensive exam.

If you did not pass the exam, you were dropped from the program. The exam was administered a couple weeks after the end of the academic year. The time allotted for the exam was three hours in the morning and three hours in the afternoon. If you did not score high enough on any part of the written exam, you were given one last chance to take an oral exam.

I passed statistics, finance and microeconomics, but had problems on the macroeconomics section and Dr. G's section. I was told I needed to attend an oral exam on those two sections. It turned out I was given my exam back and, while I needed to be prepared to answer any question asked of me, I found out the first question the faculty usually asked was if I wanted to amend my answer.

For macroeconomics, amending my answer was simple. The test question required me to graph a solution to a problem, and then discuss the answer. When I graphed my answer, I did my best to replicate the direction and slope of the two horizontal lines. But when I labeled the lines, I inadvertently flipped the descriptions. I gave the top line the label of the bottom line, and vice versa. The written discussion was based on the mislabeled lines. Effectively, my description of the solution was backwards, but I couldn't see it. So when I sat in my oral comps and was asked if I wanted to amend my answer, I easily did so.

After listening to my explanation, the economics professor asked me, "Why didn't you just answer the question right the first time?"

"Well, um, graphs are a little hard to manage when you can't see. If you flip the labels, everything else I did was one hundred percent correct."

After several audible sighs, everyone present indicated I had adequately addressed the issue, and passed me on that section of the exam.

The issue with my answer on Dr. G.'s exam was a little trickier. He asked his first question. "Would you like to amend your answer to the exam question?"

"No, I stand by the answer I gave on my exam." I was glad I could not see anyone's face. I knew my answer was correct.

"I know it is not the answer you expected based on what you taught in class, but it is a correct answer nonetheless." I paused to gather my thoughts, and then went on to give the answer he expected and to explain how the answer I gave was its statistical equivalent. There are multiple ways to run statistical tests on data that are essentially mathematical equivalents. Because Dave had taught me so thoroughly, I was well versed in multiple ways to test data. So when I'd answered Dr G.'s test question, I'd answered it using statistical methods I thought were appropriate, even though they were not what Dr. G. had taught us.

"Respectfully," I said firmly, "there is nothing wrong with my answer." The other professors in the room concurred with my explanation, and Dr. G. reluctantly gave me a passing grade. Thankfully, my second set of comprehensive exams went better.

As a PhD student, I was expected to perform the duties of a teaching assistant (TA). Mostly, that meant I had to grade accounting exams. This turned out to be a stressful responsibility. Because of my limited vision, it took me eight hours to grade what a sighted student could do in three hours. So when I had to grade, I couldn't do any of my own homework, or study for my own exams. Normally, this would not have been a problem, but undergraduate students' exam days almost always coincided with my own.

When I graded exams, I lay on the floor in my living room and put my eye against the test paper. I searched out the answers, one number at a time. I was capable of accurately performing the task, but the experience solidified my understanding of how being blind was so incredibly inefficient. And, of course, unwilling to ask for any concessions in the PhD program, the only way I knew how to overcome the inefficiency of being blind was to resign myself to working longer hours than my cohorts. I further adapted by studying for my own exams several days in advance, and hoping my memory served me well on test day.

Ultimately, I managed to get through my comprehensive exams, TA responsibilities, and, finally, the defense of my dissertation. At graduation, I'd mostly felt a sense of relief more than anything else. But there was one moment when I let myself feel the joy of my accomplishment. I had crossed the stage to receive my hood at a ceremony PhD students participate in just before graduating. Without exception, the other PhD students walked across the stage and humbly accepted their hoods. I was one of the last to be called up. When my name was announced, I used my cane to find the steps to the stage and then, once on the stage, proudly tapped my way across it. When the hood was placed in my hand, I turned and faced everyone in the auditorium. Then, I raised my arms high in the air, hood in one hand, white cane in the other, and let out a loud and joyful, "I did it!"

Though I managed to get over many hurdles as I navigated my way through the PhD program, the fear that people might judge me as less capable stayed with me. The summer before my last year in the doctoral program, I attended the national academic conference for accounting faculty in Chicago, with the sole purpose of interviewing for open tenure-track faculty positions. Prior to the meeting, I was invited to interview with the search committees from twelve schools. Still paranoid that people might subconsciously discriminate against me, I discretely held my folded white cane in my right hand whenever I met with a new group of potential employers. It was just like when I was trying to get accepted into a doctoral program. I had enough vision to navigate my way around a room, and consciously looked people square in the face to assure them I was competent. Here again, my strategy was effective. I received six invitations for further on-campus meetings. At that point, I figured anyone interested in my credentials should also know my full truth. I never hid my cane from anyone again. I received multiple job offers, and accepted a position at the University of Vermont School of Business.

Having secured my first academic position, the next hurdle I faced in transitioning from a career in business to a career in academics was how to effectively function in the classroom. As I saw it, the issue was two-pronged: how would I engage students in the classroom when I could not see their faces, and how would I manage delivering the material? Ultimately, I came up with a couple of simple tactics that served me well.

Whether I taught in a classroom large enough to accommodate sixty-five students, or in a more intimate setting with seats for thirty-five students, I still couldn't differentiate one student from another. At best, I could make out the outline of a body, but nothing more. Luckily, students are creatures of habit. Once they pick their seat on the first day of class, they usually stay in that seat for the rest of the semester. If I learned everyone's name, then I knew I could look in the general direction of a certain student, call their name, and they would respond as if I could see them. I devised a system to memorize everyone's name without using any real visual cues. Just before the start of each class, I randomly picked three students, usually sitting next to each other, to talk to. I always asked them the same four questions: what was their name, where were they from, what was their major, and what did they like to do for fun. When the discussion was over, I repeated their names. When I went back to the front of the room, I pointed in the direction of every student I had talked to up until that point in the semester, and repeated their names. Sometimes, in the classes where I had more than thirty students, I forgot a name and the student reminded me. It was a game we all enjoyed, and by the end of the semester, I usually knew everyone's name, at least as long as they didn't change seats.

While this tactic helped me call students by their correct names in the classroom, I had to remind them that when they saw me in the hallway, I could not see their faces. So if they said hello, I asked them to also say their names. Throughout the years, students often greeted me in this manner. If they forgot, I just reminded them.

"Good morning, Professor B."

"Good morning, who is that?"

"Oh yeah, sorry, it's Kevin."

"Good morning to you, too, Kevin."

Interacting with my colleagues when they passed in the hallways was a little different. I had to learn their voices in order to know who was walking by and greeting me. At first, I focused on learning the voices of the six other accounting faculty. It wasn't that hard since everyone speaks with a different volume, pitch, and accent. Once I could identify accounting faculty by voice, I made an effort to learn the voices of the ten other faculty members on my floor, and finally, the rest of the faculty housed in offices on the floor below mine. While I'd often stop and chat with my colleagues, the subject of how I was coping with all my responsibilities while not being able to see was never broached.

Back in the classroom, a second tactic enhanced my ability to teach the technical accounting and financial reporting material. I simply asked my students to be the readers of classroom materials. Effectively, they became my eyes. I always made the following announcement on the first day of class, "You need to make sure you bring your textbooks to class. We do a lot of problems in class, and the way I like to work things is we just go around the room taking turns reading problems from the book and working through them on the board."

Then on the second day of class, I picked a person at random, usually someone at one of the corner seats in the room, and that student was the first reader of the day. Then the student in the next seat was the next reader, and so on. My students learned very quickly they really did need to bring their textbooks to class, or sit next to a friend who was willing to share. Because of my systematic approach, I never had to ask for volunteers to read, or worry about how to see raised hands. If I had a question for the class, I always just asked the next student in line. Because my teaching style might put a student on the spot, they always had the option to pass if they didn't want to participate. Surprisingly, few students opted to pass.

Writing solutions to problems on the board was tricky. I'd always write on the board while standing at an angle that maximized the peripheral vision in my left eye. Accounting problems have an order to them, especially when teaching introductory financial accounting. We'd first analyze a business transaction, evaluate its impact on the financial statements, prepare the journal entry, and record the journal into in the ledger (i.e., T-Accounts in a classroom setting). The key to analyzing a business transaction was to illustrate how the financial statements stayed in balance once a transaction was recorded. So, on the left side of the blackboard, I'd write plusses and minuses under financial statement headings. Then, in the middle of the board, I'd write out the related journal entry, and then on the right side of the board, I'd show the impact of the journal entry on the T-Account. If I forgot a number from a particular problem as I moved from left to right, I simply asked the class. If I lost my place on the board, I asked the class for direction. For example, I might point to one of nine T-Accounts on the board.

"One down," someone would shout out if I were in the wrong place.

This only happened on a rare occasion, so I never felt like my credibility in the classroom was ever at risk. And the process for teaching basic accounting is the same for the entire semester. The only thing that changes is the type and complexity of the business transaction being accounted for.

Besides reading problems from the textbook, students took turns reading the PowerPoint handouts I used in the classroom. I did not project the PowerPoint materials on a screen at the front of the room. But I wanted to make sure students had a copy of what was covered in class. As students read the materials, I got my cues about the next topic I needed to cover. Teaching the accounting material itself was easy. I had years of experience in every possible aspect of the accounting profession, and was well versed in all the material taught at both the undergraduate and graduate level. I just learned to use the students to help queue up the next teaching point.

While these tactics helped keep me on track, students needed to be constantly reminded that if they had questions, they needed to speak up because I couldn't see their hands. I'm not sure I ever got the students comfortable doing this. Once, when my teaching effectiveness was being evaluated by one of my colleagues, I learned that students were still raising their hands, and waiting for me to call on them. After being given that feedback, I conscientiously stopped every couple of minutes to ask if there were any questions.

My ability to get my students to give me the cues I needed not only served me well, it also kept the students engaged in the classroom. But outside the classroom, I still had the same problem preparing for classes, grading papers, and grading exams that I had as a PhD student. It took me at least twice as long to do the same task a fully sighted person did, and that meant working most nights and weekends. I meticulously prepared and memorized material for every class session. My preparation included reviewing every single PowerPoint slide multiple times, regardless of whether, or how many times, I had previously taught the course. Even though I knew the accounting material, I could not just wing it in the classroom. I memorized the four or five main teaching topics for the day, and then, as a reminder to myself, wrote them on the upper corner of the blackboard when I entered the classroom. I familiarized myself with every accounting problem I planned to use to emphasize various teaching points, and read the online version of *Wall Street Journal* to see if anything in the current business news related to any of the accounting material previously covered in class. Most days there was something in the news I could talk about, even something as simple as a company's earnings release.

While these tactics worked for all my classes, I needed to make some adjustments when teaching advanced accounting. The advanced accounting course consisted of three main modules: consolidations, accounting for derivatives, and a little bit of governmental accounting. Consolidations took up about half the semester, and was a particularly challenging topic to teach without vision. It was the only time I asked for a TA to help me in the classroom. Even as a tenure-track professor, I seldom asked for any special accommodations. But if I felt the students' learning experience was going to be compromised, I'd let my staunch stubbornness go, and ask for the extra help.

Conceptually, doing a consolidation is simple. You take the books and records of two or more companies, combine them to show the results as if they were one single entity, and eliminate any intercompany transactions. I had worked extensively with the software that consolidated MetLife's financial statements. But there was no software in the classroom. I had to teach the students how to do this manually.

When I taught consolidations, it was the one time I did not memorize the problems we did in class. I wanted the students to experience how to think through a problem. Again, one of the beautiful things about accounting is if you do something wrong, usually the financial statements don't balance. My role in the classroom was to guide students through the process. Effectively, I only wrote on the board whatever the students told me to. If they got stuck, I'd provide technical guidance on the point. If we made a mistake, and the financial statements didn't balance, I embraced the opportunity to teach students how to troubleshoot and find the error.

The consolidation process could be distilled down to five fairly easy steps. Each step required an elimination entry that needed to be posted to the financial statements. I used the blackboard mounted on the sidewall of my classroom to write down all the elimination entries, but I could not practically use the front board to illustrate what the actual consolidated financial statements should look like. Even a simple problem required twenty to thirty rows, and five columns, of numbers to be written on the board. Instead, I developed a spreadsheet for every problem we did in class. By using spreadsheets, I was able to show each step of the five-step process. I'd set the problem up in the first tab, and then used subsequent tabs to show what the financial statements looked like when the elimination entry was posted. Once I wrote an entry on the sideboard, my TA, who worked the computer at the front of the classroom, clicked on the tab that allowed me to talk about how the consolidation entry affected the financial statements. If the entry we wrote on the board did not match the one recorded in the spreadsheet, we figured out why the two numbers did not match.

Accounting is all about repetition. Once I had taken the class through four or five consolidation problems, they got the hang of my teaching style. Then I spent the next couple of weeks increasing the complexity of the transactions being accounted for. Almost without exception, my students had a good grasp of how to perform a consolidation. On more than one occasion, I got an email from a student who faced a complex consolidation problem on the CPA exam. I never forgot the quote from one of my students: "When I saw a consolidation problem, I knew I was going to pass the exam right then and there." So, while it was not easy setting up all the problems from the textbook in spreadsheets, it certainly was rewarding.

Teaching the advanced accounting class was much easier than grading the memos I assigned as part of the workload. I held a deep conviction that accounting students needed to be capable of translating complex accounting standards into plain English, and to be good writers. So, in the advanced accounting class, students were assigned five memos during the course of the semester. Just like my days as a TA, grading written work was stressful. No longer grading papers for some other professor, I managed the workload by setting a limit on the number of memos I graded each day. While that meant it might take a full week to ten days, including Saturday and Sunday, to grade an assignment, it made the task much more manageable. This was important, since as a tenure-track professor, I still had to carve out time to do research, and perform some of the administrative duties typically assigned to faculty members.

One major advantage I had as a tenure-track faculty member came as a result of my work as a doctoral student. Even before entering the doctoral program, I understood the importance of publishing research. While my classmates were focused on doing exceptional work in the classroom, I always carved out a little time each day to work on research. Because of my work experience, I had a niche interest in examining the potential relation between managements' decisions to freeze their defined-benefit pension plans and changes in the pension accounting regulations. Two of my professors at Drexel agreed to work with me on what turned out to be two research projects. Even though I chose earnings management as my dissertation topic, the pension research projects turned into published papers when I was a tenure-track faculty member. So while doing research was another incredibly time-consuming part of my job, I had a reasonably decent portfolio of published research when it came time to prepare my case for tenure.

Proficiency in teaching, research, and service. That's what I had to establish to be granted tenured status by my colleagues. From the beginning, I accepted the challenge of meeting the same expectations as any other tenure-track faculty member. Be strong. Work hard. No distractions. My formula for moving forward served me well. I would find out if I were granted tenured status at the end of my sixth year at the university. If I were not granted tenure, I would have one year to find another position at another university.

The email from the dean of the business school came on the last day of the spring semester. The subject line read: "Congratulations." After a deep breath, I clicked to open it. Then I put my left eye an inch away from the computer monitor, and cocked my head to the right. Still struggling to see one word at a time, I read the message:

I am pleased to announce you have been promoted to Associate Professor with tenure. I will get you the signed paperwork when I get back in town next week. Congratulations.

A surge of adrenaline rushed through my body. The skin on my forearms started to tingle. I planted my elbows on my desk and dropped my face into my hands. I did it. I freakin' did it! After five years as a PhD student, and six years as an accounting professor, I'd successfully managed to build a second career after losing much of my eyesight. I immediately felt numb. Of course I'd done it. That was my way, to take a punch in the gut, and move on as though nothing happened. Be strong. Work hard. No distractions.

As I sat there, the reality of my situation started to sink in. Yes ... I did it. This was real. My mind started racing. Had it really been twelve years since I realized I was going blind? Had it really been twelve years since I left my job as a Vice President of Finance in a publicly traded company? Had I really managed to carve out two successful careers for myself? I just kept shaking my head. After another minute, I finally sat back in my chair, made my hands into fists, and raised them over my head. Tears of joy dripping down my cheeks, I mouthed the words one last time: *I did it.* I was not less capable.

Star Words

David-Elijah Nahmod

I was a happy five year old, as I recall. I was thin as a rail, and had thick, brown hair, which fell across my forehead. Even then I was a bit of a drama queen—I delighted in dramatically snapping my head back whenever my hair got into my eyes.

My parents were modern orthodox Jews. We kept a strictly kosher home and observed the Sabbath, but as "modern" orthodox, we didn't dress any differently than our non-Jewish neighbors. My parents always dressed modestly and fervently believed they were white; my dad's olive-toned complexion told a different story. All four of my grandparents had been born and raised in Damascus, Syria and spoke fluent Arabic. My grandmothers cooked Middle Eastern cuisine like kibbeh and hummus, and could belly dance. (I can still picture them swiveling their hips at weddings and bar mitzvahs, as the many gold bracelets they wore did a dance of their own, up and down their arms.)

We were Jews, but we were also Arabs. We were hardly the all-American, Caucasian family my parents fervently believed themselves to be.

Around 1961, when I was five years old, my parents took me to see *South Pacific*, my first movie. The film was a musical. I remember my excitement at being taken to the Marboro Theatre in Brooklyn, New York, where I grew up. The Marboro was an old-fashioned, single screen movie palace, which had been providing the neighborhood with entertainment since the twenties. To this day, some thirty years since I last saw a movie there, I can still clearly picture the beautiful mural of the baby blue sky that adorned the ceiling of the Marboro's spacious auditorium.

South Pacific was set on a tropical island during World War II. I believe the film was shot in Hawaii. I remember how mesmerized I was by the film's lush locations, which were a far cry from the blue-collar, urban neighborhood we lived in. Watching *South Pacific* was the first time I ever saw a palm tree.

I can only imagine what Mom and Dad must have thought when we got home from the movie. I wrapped myself in a towel and began singing "I'm Gonna Wash That Man Right Outa My Hair," one of the film's show-stopping musical numbers. My parents looked at me through confused and horrified eyes.

I was branded for life.

Not knowing what to do with their obviously effeminate son, my parents consulted a rabbi for advice, who told them I was "hyperactive." A few years later, he gave them another piece of advice, which forever changed the course of my life, and not for the better.

In 1964, at the tender age of eight, I was committed to the children's psych ward of Mount Sinai Hospital in New York City. This was what the rabbi urged them to do. My psychiatrist, Dr. Herbert J. Levowitz, seemed like a nice fellow. He was in his early thirties and wore a yarmulka at all times. After fifty years, I can no longer recall what Dr. Levowitz looked like, but I seem to remember he had a small amount of facial hair. *Did he wear glasses?* I just can't remember.

I do remember one thing quite clearly. Dr. Levowitz quoted the Torah to me—in Hebrew no less—during "therapy." He also prescribed powerful tranquilizers like Thorazine, which are now banned from use in children.

One late afternoon, another kid and I watched the *Adventures of Superman* on television in the hospital's community room. Afterward, we ran down the hallway—two eight year olds—shouting that we were flying, just like Superman. For this and this alone, we were wrestled to the ground by two muscular orderlies, who pulled our pants down and shot us up with knockout drugs. This was done to us in the common area during visiting hours. Numerous adults, including other kids' parents, stood by and did nothing while we screamed for help, tears streaming down our cheeks. Incidents like these were a regular occurrence.

What was that other kid's name? What did he look like? All I can see in my mind are fuzzy images. I seem to vaguely remember that he was Puerto Rican—New York City has always had a sizable Latino community. He and I might have become friends had we met under different, better circumstances. *I wonder how things turned out for him?* I hope he had a good life.

During my three months at Mt. Sinai, I had at least one electroshock treatment that I can remember.

When I was released from the hospital in the winter of 1965, I was an emotional wreck. The abuse I'd been subjected to continued for many years thereafter. I saw Dr. Levowitz as an outpatient for several years and was kept heavily medicated at all times. My parents never missed an opportunity to remind me how "sick" I was. There were many occasions where I would lie sprawled across the floor, begging them in tears to stop, as some of these speeches would go on for thirty to forty minutes.

At age twelve, I had an allergic reaction to one of the drugs I was given and temporarily lost fifty percent of my eyesight.

Even after this, the constant barrage of forced medication continued.

I was forced to say my prayers three times a day, according to the customs of Orthodox Judaism. I was told as a man it was my responsibility to do so. Why my father never lived up to his "responsibility" was never explained to me.

When I was in elementary school, the original *Adventures of Superman* TV series was one of my favorite shows. WPIX TV in New York ran the series every afternoon at 4 p.m. I always felt excited and happy when it was time for the show to come on. I didn't have very many happy moments during those years. After a few weeks, my mother told me I could no longer watch *Superman*. Instead, I had to say my afternoon prayers at 4 p.m.

"Why can't I say them at 3:30?" I asked.

Mom went into one of her bizarre tirades, "explaining" to me that because of the angle of the sun in relation to the earth, 4 p.m. was the apex of the afternoon, so therefore I had to say my prayers at 4 p.m., or God would decline to accept them. Over the years, everything I enjoyed, everything that gave me pleasure, was taken away from me for reasons like this. I was not allowed to be happy, ever.

Through it all, horror movies like *Dracula Has Risen From the Grave* and *The Vampire Lovers* were my solace, my escape. When I was able to get out of the house and get to the movies to see films such as these, I was able to enjoy myself for a few hours. I was able to escape from the real life horrors of the world I lived in.

As I entered my twenties, I knew something was terribly wrong. I wasn't like other people. I was nervous and high strung. I had no attention span. I struggled to look people in the eye when I spoke to them. I was sad most of the time. I even had blackouts during which I would have manic episodes that I can barely remember.

When I felt manic, I would speak rapidly and was often unable to stop. I couldn't sit in the house, so I would go on long walks, walking quickly, sometimes whispering aloud to myself (I didn't always realize that I was doing this). I would yell at people at the slightest provocation, sometimes unaware of what I had done until after the fact. Sitting still was impossible. Sometimes I would pace around my apartment for hours on end --reading a book or watching a film on TV was impossible. I would lie awake at night, unable to sleep. When I finally slept, I would have horrific nightmares in which I died or in which people tried to hurt me. I would often wake up shaking. Sometimes I would be on the verge of tears—for days on end.

How I got through those years remains a mystery to me. I lost many jobs and many friends because of the state I was in.

Around age thirty, I realized what the source of my trouble was. I cut my family out of my life and never looked back. My mother tried to contact me several times over the next dozen or so years, but I refused to let her back in. I couldn't take anymore of her, or of a community that would never allow me to be myself. I was sick. I was exhausted. I yearned for a better life.

In my forties, I was diagnosed with post-traumatic stress disorder (PTSD), the result of my horrific childhood. I didn't need a doctor to tell me what had caused this.

I did have some minor, on-again off-again contact with my cousin Miriam after that. In 2013, the last time we spoke, Miriam told me my mother had passed away the year before. According to Miriam, my mom went to her grave with no real understanding as to why we hadn't spoken for the past twenty-five years, though she had admitted, albeit grudgingly, that she had made "a few mistakes."

Even today I have nightmares, flashbacks and anxiety attacks that are related to my horrific childhood. But now

I take the right medication and, for the most part, the symptoms are under control. Yet even today, I'm unable to deal with large crowds.

In 1999, my friend Joe began talking about *Passions*, a new daytime soap opera he had recently begun watching. "You have to watch it," he said. "It's the kind of show you'd love."

One afternoon, I decided to check out an episode of *Passions* and found a delightful guilty pleasure.

Passions was a mad satire of traditional soap opera conventions, classic horror movies and retro pop culture. One particularly memorable storyline featured Tabitha (Juliet Mills) and Timmy (Josh Ryan Evans) visiting the Bates Motel, where they met Norma Bates (Marianne Muellerleile), the axe-wielding lesbian sister to Norman Bates, the mad killer from Alfred Hitchcock's *Psycho*. Tabitha was a three-hundred-year-old witch. Timmy was a doll she had brought to life.

I wrote a letter to the editor of *Scary Monsters Magazine*, a retro-themed print publication I had begun reading, and suggested they do a feature on *Passions*. Much to my surprise, I received a personal reply. Imagine my delight at being told by editor/publisher Dennis Druktenis that I had a strong and impressive writing style. He asked me to do the story.

With no previous journalism experience, I called NBC Studios in Hollywood and asked to be put in contact with *Passions'* publicity rep. I'm sure they were amused by me, as I had no idea what I was doing. I was winging it. But I was determined to get onto the set of that show and interview the cast.

I didn't think my request would be granted, but it was. In late 2001, I traveled to Los Angeles to meet the cast of *Passions*. I was so determined to see this assignment through that I paid for my own airfare, which was a good bit more than the paltry $200 fee I would be paid for writing the story. I didn't care. I seemed to sense on a gut level that if I did a good job and saw this story published, it might lead to bigger and better things for me.

I felt as though I were dreaming as I signed in at the NBC TV studio gates. I was in Hollywood. I was the guest of a Hollywood studio. I was about to meet some very famous actors. This was all part of a professional writing assignment, which came my way quite unexpectedly. Was my lifelong dream to be part of the entertainment industry coming true?

There was only one small problem: my anxieties; my deep-rooted fear of meeting new people and of being in large groups, and my inability to feel safe around people I don't know. But I was determined to get this assignment done. I was determined to see my piece published, and so, as I was led to the set of *Passions*, I said a little prayer.

What I know now, but didn't know then, is that I'm disabled. I never thought of myself as disabled up until that time. I have all five of my senses. I could walk, run, ride my bicycle and do heavy lifting with ease. I'm not disabled!

My closest friend, who is totally blind, made me realize the denial I was living in. Post-traumatic stress disorder, more commonly known as PTSD, is one of the conditions covered by the Americans with Disabilities Act, the groundbreaking federal law that prohibits discrimination in jobs, housing and public accommodations on the basis of disability. My PTSD has been quite debilitating at times. If that were not the case, I would have had no problem walking onto the set of *Passions* and chatting with the cast.

So there I was in Hollywood, inside NBC's production studios, about to meet the cast of *Passions*. How in the world was I going to get past my anxieties, conduct those interviews and get the story done? At this point, I was well aware of the difficulties I faced in meeting new people and in feeling safe in groups of strangers. I prayed that things would go well. My friend Joe, who lives in Hollywood, came along to serve as my photographer. I had known Joe for over twenty years. He was a good friend and his presence was a comfort.

Joe and I were seated as, one by one, cast members from *Passions* were brought over and introduced to us. One of the first was Jesse Metcalfe, who played the hunky and heroic Miguel Lopez Fitzgerald. Metcalfe went on to star in a number of films. He also had a recurring role on the primetime series *Desperate Housewives,* and played Bobby Ewing's son on TNT's reboot of the eighties series *Dallas.* He was a dazzlingly beautiful man, muscular, with a beautiful, olive-skinned complexion and jet-black hair. He was the kind of guy whose eyes and teeth seemed to sparkle when he smiled. He was also quite self-confident. I felt instantly intimidated by him. I could hear my voice quivering as I shook his hand and asked him a few questions.

Easy does it, I told myself. He was being friendly and polite. He was answering my questions, and the quotes were great. He wasn't going to bite me. *Just write down whatever he says and thank him.* Could he see my leg shaking? Could he hear the nervous quiver in my voice? I sure hoped not.

Next came Jade Harlow, a longhaired actress in her late teens who was thrilled about her job on the show. Jade wasn't just an actress, she was a fan. She squealed with delight when I told her I was doing a story for a magazine called *Scary Monsters.*

"I love horror movies!" she exclaimed, as she showed Joe and I the DVD box set of the *A Nightmare on Elm Street* movies she had just gotten. *I like her*, I thought. *A sweet young soul mate!* Jade's effervescent personality and her enthusiasm for her work helped put me at ease.

But my fears came rushing back as I spotted Juliet Mills approaching us. I loved Mills' delicious, over-the-top performances as the witchy Tabitha. Mills herself clearly relished the role.

Mills is a scion of British theater royalty. (Her dad, Sir John Mills, was considered to have been one of England's greatest actors.) Then in her sixties, Mills had been considered quite a beauty in her younger years. She had long, blonde, curly hair, an aristocratic demeanor and a lovely, elegant British accent. Though obviously an older woman, much of her beauty remained intact.

I was thrilled to meet Juliet Mills, but I was also terrified. I felt intimidated by all she represented and found it difficult to make eye contact with her. My anxieties nearly overwhelmed me as I spoke to her—I could feel a manic attack looming on my horizon.

Get your shit together, I told myself. *You have been granted a privilege in being allowed to come here. Don't fuck it up.*

Mills was wonderful. She dazzled me with tales of her magical childhood, which included being taken shopping in London by her Godmother, the actress Vivien Leigh (*Gone With the Wind*).

Okay, that went well after all, thank God. Who's next?

Next up was Josh Ryan Evans, the young actor who played Timmy, the doll that had been brought to life by Tabitha's witchcraft. Though he was about to turn twenty years old, Josh had the appearance and voice of a small child due to being born with achondroplasia, a form of dwarfism. His condition had caused him to be plagued with health problems for his entire life, and I believe he knew he wasn't long for this world. But that didn't stop him from pursuing his dream. He and Mills were *Passions'* most popular performers. Evans had also appeared on several episodes of the primetime TV series *Ally McBeal*, and in the movie *The Grinch*, among other roles.

I was shocked at how frail he was. He extended his hand to greet me, and I was almost afraid to reach out to him, out of fear I might hurt him. I'm six feet tall and was about one hundred and seventy five pounds at the time. Evans was a petite little thing. Thin as a rail, he stood a little over three feet high. He climbed onto a chair with his arms, much the way a child would.

"Do you need any help?" I asked him.

"No, I'm fine," he said. "I'm Josh. How are you?"

I asked him what he liked about working on *Passions*. It was a dream come true, he told me. He and Mills were the defacto stars of the show. The campy, over-the-top chemistry of their two characters was the primary reason three million viewers were tuning in every afternoon. After a few minutes of talking about the show, Josh asked me if I lived in Hollywood.

"No, I flew in from the East Coast to do this," I said. "I live in the New York City area."

He began talking about the 9/11 terrorist attacks, which had happened just a month earlier. He spoke quite eloquently of his heartbreak over the massive loss of life. He asked me if everyone I knew was okay.

"I heard a few people in my neighborhood were killed," I said. "But everyone I know is fine."

"I'm glad to hear that," he said.

This was not the conversation I expected to have. This frail little guy touched me very deeply. For the first time that day, I felt truly at ease. I had five more interviews to do, and I breezed right through them. On the flight home the next day, I found myself thinking of Josh.

"Dream big," the little guy told us. Josh dreamed

big and lived large. He died of heart disease at age twenty, less than a year after I met him. But he lived long enough to overcome his disability and see his dreams come true. All these years later, Josh Ryan Evans remains one of the people that most inspires me.

***

If he could overcome his disability, then I could overcome mine.

Back in Hoboken, NJ, where I lived at the time, I sat in the back room of my three-room apartment on Adams Street, in the room I called my "office," and got to work on my story. First, I described to the *Scary Monsters* readership why a daytime soap opera was being featured in a monster movie magazine. I described the mad adventures of Tabitha and Timmy, which, in addition to visiting the Bates Motel, included conjuring up demons and casting spells intended to bring "pain and suffering" on the unsuspecting residents of Harmony, Maine. I recounted the hilariously campy storyline in which the love-struck teenager Kay Bennett stole a book of spells from Tabitha's house so she could magically make the hunky Miguel love her. The inexperienced Kay botched her freshman attempt at witchcraft, accidentally zapping her and her cousin Charity into the flaming pits of hell. Miguel, of course, had to jump through an inter-dimensional portal so he could rescue the ladies.

This wasn't *As the World Turns*.

Throughout my piece, I sprinkled quotes I had gotten from the various *Passions* cast members I'd spoken to. The story was published in late 2001. Much to my surprise, it was well received by the twenty thousand or so people who read *Scary Monsters*. In early 2002, I was offered my own column in the magazine. I called the column "Scary Reviews." In each issue, I reviewed an average of three to four horror films as they were released on DVD or Blu Ray. I still do that column today.

In 2003, I decided to move back to San Francisco, where I had lived during the eighties. I sent a few sample columns of "Scary Reviews" to the editors of *Bay Area Reporter*, a weekly LGBT news publication with a six-figure readership. I had my first assignment from them before I even arrived in town. I'm still writing for the *Bay Area Reporter*—hard news, film reviews, celebrity interviews, previews of special events. I do it all. I also contribute regularly to LGBT publications in Colorado and South Florida. In 2014, I began contributing to *Hoodline*, a general news publication in San Francisco. And in January 2017, I was invited to join the writing staff of *SF Sounds*, a new arts and culture magazine that serves the San Francisco Bay Area. I no longer have what's called a "day job"; writing has become my career, my primary income source.

In 2012, I won an award. I was named "Best Film Reviewer" at the Rondo Hatton Classic Horror Film Awards for my work on the "Scary Reviews" column. My little award statue, with my name on its plaque, occupies a place of honor on my bookshelf.

All this came into being, not because of that first letter I wrote to *Scary Monsters Magazine*, but because I forced myself to overcome my fears and anxieties in order to get the job I was given done. I wrote a few words about stars that graciously gave me a few moments of their time and launched a career I never expected.

"Pour yourself a drink, put on some lipstick, and pull yourself together," Elizabeth Taylor said during a particularly difficult period of her life. Sometimes the most simplistic thoughts are the wisest.

My personal demons continue to haunt me. I still live with PTSD. I still have bouts of depression and anxiety attacks. In recent times, I've needed police intervention—after a woman in Delaware harassed me and began contacting my friends, because I wrote something she "disapproved" of. Her actions went on for several years—there were hundreds of incidents. She brought my PTSD levels roaring back. Most recently, I endured depressions so severe it affected my ability to work. Over the past two years, I began to suffer recurring incidents of short-term memory loss. My doctor told me this was caused from the stress of dealing with my stalker. I've had to go back on medication.

My friend was right. I am indeed disabled.

But I'm determined to hold onto this new career I've built up and love. There were days when I wasn't emotionally well enough to talk, so I asked interview subjects if we could conduct the interview via email. I pretended to be too ill with the flu or laryngitis as an explanation for why I couldn't talk on the phone. A number of rather famous people kindly complied. I wonder what they would have thought if I told them the truth—that I was in the midst of a severe anxiety attack and was too frightened to talk to them.

One day I was offered an interview with Jennifer Hudson, the Oscar-winning star of the film *Dreamgirls*. Hudson had since gone on to win a number of other awards and had become a major star in the music world. She had a new album out and was going to spend an entire day giving thirty-minute phone interviews with one journalist after another. The fact I was chosen spoke well of my reputation and the work I had done. Email was not an option. Once again, I was going to have to get past my anxieties and get the job done. As before, I knew I could not afford to fuck this up.

About five minutes before my scheduled time, the phone rang. "Ms. Hudson is finishing up with *The Hollywood Reporter*," I was told. "Please hold the line."

"Thank you," I managed in a shaky voice.

A few minutes later, I heard the phone click. "Hi, this is Jennifer. Is this David?"

"Hi Jennifer, I'm so honored to speak to you," I said.

Uh, oh. That was dumb, I thought.

I asked her to describe her feelings on the night she won her Oscar and about her experience singing at Michael Jackson's memorial service. Her answers were clear, concise and detailed ... which should have set me at ease, but didn't. I felt overwhelmed by my ongoing anxieties, and by the fact I was on the phone with a major, award-winning celebrity. I could hear my voice shaking. I felt a major anxiety attack coming on, and I could not afford to let that happen. Once again, I had been granted a privilege. I had been granted an interview with an Oscar-winning movie and recording star. I had to hold it together.

Okay, I told myself. *If I can hear the nervous quiver in my voice, then Ms. Hudson can hear it, too. Don't pretend it isn't happening, that'll just make me look stupid.*

"So I have to fess up," I said to Ms. Hudson. "I'm a big fan of yours—I loved your work in *Dreamgirls* and I love your voice, so I'm a little nervous speaking with you. I guess I'm just a star struck kid."

"And that's okay, baby," Jennifer Hudson said cheerfully.

Wow, I thought. *That was great!*

She set me at ease and we continued the interview. A few minutes later, Hudson's press rep cut into the call.

"Two minutes to go," the publicist said. Another interviewer was waiting to speak to Hudson, and my time with her was about done. I asked her one more question.

"Thank you for your time," I said as our chat drew to a close. "You can expect a great story from me."

"Thank you, David," she said. "It was really nice talking to you."

To date, Jennifer Hudson is the only person I've interviewed that's ever said that to me.

My interview with Hudson was published in the *Bay Area Reporter* and *South Florida Gay News*. It turned out to be quite a nice little piece. I felt pleased with myself. Once again, I had overcome my anxieties, my often-overwhelming fear of strangers, and had gotten the job done.

So how am I doing these days? As with any chronic condition, my PTSD comes and goes. I have good days and bad days. Stories written by me are published several times a week. Numbers on my Facebook author page are up. News, entertainment, nightlife, I cover it all, and I love every minute of doing so, regardless of how my health is doing.

As I write this, the Christmas/Chanukah/New Year's holidays are upon us. I received my invitation to the annual holiday parties from *Bay Area Reporter* and *Hoodline*. I had not been to *Bay Area Reporter's* party in nearly five years because of my anxieties—my innate fear of crowds and of meeting strangers. Yesterday, I confided to a *Hoodline* editor and told him the truth about why I was hesitant to attend.

"I really hope to see you there," he said. "Just sit in a corner and I'll get you a drink."

After thinking it over, I decided to go to both parties. These publications have been very supportive of me over the years; they stood up for me above and beyond the call of duty and gave me the career I want. I love what I do for them. I have every right to celebrate that. I'm going to go and have a great time. I deserve that.

And so I went. As with my visit to the set of *Passions* and my phone call with Jennifer Hudson, I was nervous. But I was going to a party, not a prison cell. If the going got rough, I could always leave.

At both parties, I was warmly greeted. At the *Bay Area Reporter* party, a local performer I had interviewed, but had never met—a lesbian comic who's act included impersonating *Star Trek's* William Shatner—hugged me and thanked me for the good coverage I had given her. At the *Hoodline* party, the editor who urged me to attend smiled and said he was glad to see me. There were moments at both parties where I had to struggle a bit in order to keep up with the conversation, but, for the most part, everything went well.

Once again, I took a deep breath, did what I wanted to do, and found out I could do more than I gave myself credit for.

I now find myself thinking of little Josh Ryan Evans, who never let his disability stop him from pursuing his goals. His dreams came true, and now, so are mine.

Firsts in Art
Kimberly Gerry-Tucker

Whether I'm gluing puzzle pieces into an art collage, attempting a new art medium, or even saving high resolution photographs of my paintings to the proper DPI, I ask myself: What are the best methods? What possible scenarios can I expect? What can go wrong? Are there various ways to try each thing, and which will be best for **me**? How is this activity going to be uniquely mine? What are the rules?

As a child, I would spend hours on detailed pencil sketches. I drew trees, plants, still lifes, cartoons. I would sometimes draw my own imaginary wrestlers complete with "flaws" (inspired by a Bugs Bunny episode I adored called "The Crusher"). One wrestler I drew had exaggerated muscles, a big funny nose, and had an aversion to peaches, like my father who didn't like the sensory feel of them. I drew my wrestler's opponent, a skinny guy in one-piece wresting attire who secretly brought a peach into the ring to defeat the burly guy twice his size . . . Know thy friends, but know thine enemies, too! I still have many of these drawings today.

I like to say I was born "the seventh child of the seventh child," because this sounds poetic. I really *was* the seventh child, born to a woman who had a half dozen children and decided to give me, the seventh, up for adoption. Whether my birth mother was a "seventh" child I don't know, but I pretend she was. At three days old, I was in the arms of my adoptive mother, who stood on the porch stoop to receive me from Nina, a family member who was the middle person in the private adoption. She exclaimed, "She's mine! My baby! My own baby!"

She tells me later that in that moment her dreams for my future played in her head: I'd be blond like she was, a cheerleader, and an athlete. There were times growing up I felt I was not at all what she expected, like when she would take the black crayon away from me and hand me a yellow one. "Why do you color all the Mommies with black hair?" she'd ask. "Can you color *one* with blond hair?" Or years after her death, when my father said this to me, "I asked your mother if she wanted to adopt a second time and she said no, because when you adopt someone else's child, you never know what you'll get."

Unlike me, my mother *was* athletic, easy to laugh. I was dark and tall, she short and fair. My eyes were the color of treetops, and hers, blue flannel. She loved to sing (aptly she was named Carol), where I struggled to have a voice at all. Nicknamed Tank, my middle-aged mother enjoyed football games with siblings. I sat in a quiet place, sometimes in a closet with a bare bulb hanging above my head, to study and catalog rocks, to read autobiographies from the library, and, of course, to draw.

She taught me patience, kindness, loyalty to family, unbounded love for children and animals. The swirls in the linoleum of our apartment and on our water-stained walls in silhouettes like swans, were, to me, endless beauty, **art**—the backdrop to our daily lives, in the same way that TV sitcoms had sailboat paintings on the walls of orange and green designer living rooms. Our props were piles of "clutter," as she was a hoarder. In the piles, I saw objects d'art. In all the glorious manifestations of dust, I saw nature's sculptures. I stared at the dust, not unlike someone having an absence seizure. Unlike the ordered TV sitcom sets that were so mysterious to me, there was no canned laughter in our home; it was real and it was in abundance.

In the boards of my childhood porch, which ran distortedly away from me in a thought provoking perspective, I was reminded of the painting of Van Gogh's bedroom I had seen in a book. In our black cat's angular jaw, I saw Monet's charismatic cat portraits. I walked around the corner of my house once and saw a pile of unidentifiable Cubist shapes in an interesting arrangement. After a minute, my eyes picked out that it was the familiar picnic table.

Incredibly clumsy, I often barked my legs on corners and was continually mapping my way through my environment, unable to step on the black parts of our linoleum, and avoiding certain textures altogether, like those atrocious vinyl kitchen chairs! I would stand on those chairs and allow her to dress me for school, but only if she kept her eyes closed. I couldn't do tiny buttons, as I seemed to have little dexterity, except for when there was a pencil in my hand. If she opened her eyes, I'd scream. I preferred to sit under the table and practice my tying skills while I ate my food, with the shoelace tied to the table leg by my mother, because she ingeniously had decided if I were to take my meals there, she'd give me something useful to do.

To the trees of my youth I assigned names like Mother Pine, Mid-Aged Man, Garbage Bush, or Butterfly Tree. The boulders around the trees where He (or She?) put them were castles I swept with tree arms. In the spring, caterpillars crawled the exterior of our three-family house. I would stare at the grey peeling paint, and the caterpillar moving along past those dry paint curls became mini buildings, I thought, from its perspective. I blurred my eyes so I saw every color there is—*inside* the swirls of grey—and the caterpillar itself was a train passing through it all.

While other kids played with each other, I stretched out cat-like on truck-sized boulders and picked mica all day; even the smoky black kind. I adjusted my elbows, which fit into rock armrests. Pin-dot-sized red insects mesmerized me, gliding over the rock terrain. I had super vision, of course, so I could see them waving their flags and bagpipes. I could hear them. The alive speck-dots had adventurous missions to get on with—over the moss-stained crannies, and sparkly pink and clear quartz deposits. Nevertheless, sometimes I was evil and ended their lives with a fingertip.

I had a childhood neighbor my age that, because of close proximity, was my (one) friend, the only kid nearby. We lived by a four-lane highway near a sandbank where rats played. A dense thicket (playground!) nearby was a dumping ground for refrigerators and old TVs where we "kept house," and made wood and dandelion pretend salads in broken light fixtures for bowls. She wore cat eye glasses and a back brace for severe scoliosis. In our own ways, we both stood out as being unique.

When we moved across town into public housing, I had trouble leaving behind the rocks, broken glass, and grapevines; and wanted to take along every grain of sand, and every favorite path, along with me to the new house. I still have a vial by my bedside of Special Dust—*crushed sparkling mica* from the faces of my childhood boulders. I suppose where others saw trash I saw possibilities. Beauty.

I grew up in "The Valley" in New Haven County, Connecticut surrounded by humble hills, with a river flowing through it that picks up salt water from an ocean inlet. I find this small town background in equal measure satisfying and disappointing. I would put paper bags on my arms and jump from the picnic table, wanting so badly to fly out over the hills and into the mysterious world of cityscapes I'd seen in travel brochures and books. Yet my heart seemed rooted to the place where I could roam riverbanks on excursions with my father, and find, with my poles and nets in its deep ebbs and flows, the exotic mix of salt and fresh water life.

I wish now, in retrospect, I was put in a specialized classroom where I could've gotten attention, with a better teacher-to-student ratio. But I was mainstreamed, and in the seventies, autism was not on the radar like it is today. My diagnosis would not come until adulthood, during the process of diagnosing my son with autism. While my childhood artwork drew attention from my peers (I often had a small group gathered to peer over my shoulder), my differentness drew attention, too. In school, I stared at the pattern the radiators made, having to tune out the sensory stimuli of children laughing and rustling in waves of sound, for me to properly absorb lessons. Kids passed their hands in front of my face, "Is there anybody in there? Yoo-hoo!" I adored learning, but the environment conflicted with the process.

I saw many specialists growing up, but often during a session one on one, I would see the tape recorder on the table and be unable to say a single word. I would not give my voice to just anyone, and still many relatives today have not heard the sound of me speaking. When I had crying, hiccoughing, hyperventilating meltdowns, my mother knew to turn down the lights and rock me in a deep-pressure, mama-bear hug until I came to myself. She immersed me in extracurricular activities from an early age, to draw me out of my muteness. And although I know she couldn't quite understand my differentness, she never belittled me for it. While the socializing and friend-making aspect of catechism, Girl Scouts or 4-H escaped me, the whittling, candle making and crafts entranced me. I remember happily making paper roses, systematically, one after the other, hundreds without pausing, and then affixing them to a huge flatbed truck, working until after midnight for the parade the next day. The only drawback being, I had agreed to sit on the float as it went down Main Street and wave mechanically to people. I did this as promised, and I got to look at the paper roses surrounding me as I did so, and I remembered, smiling, the pleasure I enjoyed in making them, as I waved robotically to the crowd.

I believe I was placed, in some divine way, in the right little family—*for me*. I was loved unconditionally, I was supported, I was encouraged, I was not physically abused, and I was supplied with art supplies. If I had none on hand, I collected chewing gum wrappers to fold into sculptures for hours on end, or busied myself in assigning new uses for the items found in our piles. Sometimes I was allowed, under supervision, to melt crayons over bottles in streams of flowing colors, with the aid of a burning candle. Once, I watched, puzzled, as my father turned over couch cushions for spare change, and I saw him bottom up, digging in the car seats for money. Though we lived a spare existence, he found a way to buy me the microscope he knew I wanted. I spent hours in my closet examining slides of spit and boogers, Elm leaves and scabs! My father would arrive after work and throw down his dented lunch pail, calling, "I'm home, you lucky people!" I did feel lucky. What other parents had the patience to make me the *same* meal, every day, for decades!?

I quit school as soon as I could, at the age of sixteen. This was due, in no small part, to the bullying. While I felt the art lessons were just getting good, and I knew I would miss them, I didn't know how to handle the boys on the other bus who held up signs: "Are you deaf, dumb or just stupid?" My father punched a hole in the wall the day I quit, but I was compelled to teach myself whatever I was inspired to learn. By no means was my education over. From now on, it would be on my terms though. My mother signed me up for classes and we earned our GEDs together. These classes were easy academically for me, but socially, not so much. I remember the teacher pausing at my desk and pondering aloud about me, "She's like an unemotional Sphynx." Over the next few years, I took a few correspondence courses through the mail, too—one for art, which I never completed, due to financial circumstance, and one in writing.

I would marry the first boy who asked me. We enjoyed music, hiking, and animals, but he did not share my need to create. At tag sales he looked for tools and collectibles. I looked for art ideas. I found supplies at flea markets. Finding plates in primary colors was a treat. I remember when the flea market guy said, "Let me give you a discount on those. They're chipped."

I said, "It doesn't matter. I'll pay the full price. I plan to break them anyway to do mosaics." Oh, I caught hell and a lecture for that from my husband who was a shrewd haggler by nature. I was not!

I bought chipped plates full price from that flea market table. I smashed them under a sheet so the pieces wouldn't fly into an eye. Then the shards were sorted into groups. If one had a red fleck, into the red bits container it went. If a shard had greens in it, into the green bits container it went, and so on . . . I bought some grout and built mosaics on everything from remote control holders to plant pots. Each "broken" piece had a proper place in the scheme of things, no matter how seemingly insignificant. Once my husband came home from work and stopped frozen in the living room, as he was about to put down his thermos. Seeing the entire entertainment center covered in mosaics, he shook his head and scolded me, "Why do you ruin everything?" But I saw the amused grin he tried so hard to hide. Interestingly enough, though he would grouse about my art projects, he was the first to bring out my creations when his family came to visit, the first to praise my art and show it off to people.

When I first decided to paint in my mid-twenties, I knew I would measure success not by whether or not I "sold" anything. Oh no! I never ever planned on showing anyone my stuff. I knew I would measure success by how painting *felt*. Right away I knew something was going on in my brain when I painted—a therapeutic and cleansing sort of thing. I soon learned through my research that my brain was going into a theta wave state while immersed in artistic activity. After a painting session, it seemed I was probably benefitting from the experience in much the same way a person benefits from meditation, a yoga session, or for some people: time spent socializing with friends. That is not something I did much. If anxiety was a thorn, then painting not only metaphorically removed it, but was a much-needed salve, too! It soon became a necessary thing to do.

I always think of this in terms of a cooking pot my mother owned, which had a hole in the lid that rattled. I was fascinated by it and loved watching the little hole vent steam in the cooking process. Painting is that vent hole, for me.

I suppose I should have known painting was a natural thing for me to try. Art class was always my favorite class in school, and I sometimes won plaques, ribbons or awards. In sixth grade, I was one of six children selected to help with a bicentennial mural on a wall outside our school. This activity should've fueled an interest in painting, right? It *didn't,* because although I enjoyed being outside while the rest of the class was inside, my need to *know* all about painting was *missing* from this experience. We were not taught about Van Gogh's love for his beloved paint supplies. We, at the age of twelve, had not really been taught technique. Now we were *not* given brushes suited for rendering of detail in this mural, and so my first real painting attempt on this wall felt futile. The brushes were . . . clunky. I stood there listening to the other five kids laugh, joke with each other, finish the branch of someone else's tree, and just plain view this as a group activity. A shared thing.

That was unnatural to me. A teacher would come by and say, "It's a bicentennial painting, remember. You will paint a drum. We want it to be blue. Who would like to paint the drumsticks after Kim paints the drum?"

There would be five hands in the air: "Me! Me!"

This shared experience did not *feel* good to me. It put me off to painting really, because it felt uncomfortable. My mind was not engaged—just my *hands,* which seemed a separate part of me. There was no connection there. You might say that other than the typical art classes in school where I was given a sheet of white paper and a useless brush that didn't roll to a point like a Beagle dog's tail, and told to paint flowers, this shared mural was my first painting endeavor. But I don't count the school mural as my first real painting, because I was disconnected from the experience.

So it was in my twenties I became very interested in not only artists, but also their *lives*. Up to this point, I was doing other art: quilling pictures made by rolling colored paper into curls and gluing them onto paper. Decoupage projects, too. I often amassed brochures, old magazines and picture books from flea markets to tear and glue scenes onto bureau drawers, art supply cabinets and boxes. I liked sewing elves, too, from snips of discarded fabric, and bits and pieces I found in my cellar. I had taught myself to sew doll clothes when I was eleven, so this came naturally.

For a few years in my twenties, I helped my mother with painting faces on her ceramic pieces, which we would donate to the Ronald McDonald House charity. My mother and I would also visit with a co-worker of my mother's, and spend time in her charming craft room, just the three of us. They would chat as the three of us busily used glue guns, and all manner of craft items, making Christmas ornaments. I even went to a few ceramic classes with my mother and did some of my own ceramic pieces. I had a knack for painting shadows and highlights into the statues.

My containers of mosaic pieces, sorted by color, wound up in a big, old, green, satin-lined suitcase. I *loved* the feel of grout on my bare fingers—creamy, cold and white. I had done all of these artistic activities, and many, many more, by the time I was twenty-five.

During this time of my life, I had collected at least a dozen books on art, and I had subscribed to a few art-focused magazines as well. I found I liked to cut out the pictures and use them for decoupage, and I loved reading about the artists' inspirations, methods, lifestyles, and materials of choice. I was not painting though as a past time, as yet. I was completely enamored with reading Van Gogh's letters to his brother Theo (all available not only in my books, but online, too), because I was *relating* to the artists, I was *connecting* to their reasons for creating. And that learning was enough.

I was reading about Gauguin's trips to the tropics. I was studying Picasso's blue period, wondering about Dali's inspirations, and learning about Da Vinci's fascinating life. I have always spent a lot of time reading—having read the set of encyclopedias at a young age, for fun—so I had a strong idea who these painters were. My books of choice were historical nonfiction, horror, and especially memoir. (Still my choices.) I liked knowing what made people tick, to coin a figure of speech. Learning about people like Frida Kahlo, Degas and Monet (but especially Vincent van Gogh) was a mix of two of my interests: human behavior and the arts. I was beginning the study, the research, the connection to art I mentioned here, and yet I didn't know that at the time. In sixth grade, painting had come to me and I hadn't felt it. But now, now *I* was coming to painting and I didn't even consciously realize it. My interest led me. And I didn't even really own any paint supplies yet, other than a few detail brushes and bottles of ceramic paint I used for the charity crafts and Christmas ornaments.

I had bought canvas on a whim and received some for Christmas, too; so I dabbled a little in self- portrait, but these exercises were really a "getting acquainted" phase. I was seeing what the brush could do in regard to how viscous the paint was, and by varying the ways I held the brushes and how much water, or pressure, was applied. These little paintings went into a closet next to my childhood sketches—kind of forgotten and soon gathering dust.

One Sunday, I was walking through the biggest flea market in New England: Elephant's Trunk, in New Milford, CT. It was my opportunity to collect pottery for smashing—to do my mosaics. I was also on the lookout for items that would fill my various collections. At this point I had several collections going: wooden sailors, African American figurines, salt and pepper shakers, and cat statues, to name a few. On one of the tables I remember I spotted a woodworking handsaw, the type of muscle-powered saw used to cut wood into shapes. It had a simple wooden handle into which a few decorative touches had been designed. I would later go on to woodcarving with a Hungarian mentor and fine artist who became a very dear friend, but at this point, I knew very little about woodworking tools. I did however know that this handsaw was unique for a couple of reasons: it was definitely an antique, and it had a quaint landscape painted artfully across the blade!

My husband was ten paces ahead—perusing baseball cards, and chatting up a seller for a good price. I was alone at the table with the handsaw and its seller, a middle-aged woman, who smiled a greeting at me. I did my best to mirror that greeting. I surveyed all the other wares she had laid out: tea cups and saucers, costume jewelry, dusty knick-knacks . . . but my gaze kept returning to the painted saw blade. I picked it up.

Before I could ask any questions, she read my mind and said, "I got that at a tag sale in Pennsylvania a few years ago. I've had it hanging in my kitchen ever since. Painting farm scenes on cabinets and saw blades is pretty big in Pennsylvania."

I nodded politely, set the blade back down, and hurried to catch up with my husband. I asked him to walk back to the table and check out the saw blade. He was not exactly an appreciator of art, but I wanted him to see it. He checked it out and walked up to me.

"Yeah, that was an interesting thing to paint on," he said. We continued our walk through the flea market.

"I can do that," I said offhandedly, twenty minutes later.

"What?" he asked.

"That saw blade back there. I can *do* that."

"Yeah I'm sure you could," he said. "So later we'll get you some blades."

***

And so after trips to Home Depot for blades and Koenig's for paint and brushes, my first real painting came about! It was a gray barn with a broken down tractor in front of it, overgrown with weeds. Of course it was a barn. I had a deep calling to barns, especially the dilapidated ones, the ones with light showing through worn boards. I had developed not only an appreciation for them as sentinels of the past, but had a sense of mourning for them as they disappeared from America's landscape. I wanted to preserve them in paint! I wanted to plan out a serious barn book, complete with detailed interviews with barn owners and locations and histories of each barn's life. I wanted to travel up and down the New England coast taking pictures of these relics, painting them for posterity, interviewing and logging info, and putting my barn paintings into a calendar or a beautifully illustrated (with my paintings and photos) barn book! A discouraging routine trip to Barnes and Noble revealed that my idea had already been done and so this thought was abandoned, but I continued to immerse myself in saw paintings.

Surprisingly, these early paintings came naturally to me. I would paint for eight hours straight, forgetting to eat and sitting on my foot to hold in my pee. Eventually, I learned pacing! My first real painting was on a circular saw blade. I planned out the painting to accommodate the hole in the middle.

As I well suspected, there were learning curves; the lessons I explained earlier, which are *learned through doing*. For example, I found that brand new blades sometimes had a coating of oil that needed to be scrubbed off and dried thoroughly. I learned to protect the blades with an under-spray of gray automobile primer (available in the automotive section of department stores), to protect against rust and help the paint adhere. I learned after attempting to use lovely, rich, creamy, and vibrant oil paint, that it was not my medium of choice for blades. Acrylics became my preferred choice. Not only did I not like the smell of turpentine for oil paint cleanup, but my brain began to play out worst possible scenarios: what if turpentine rags spontaneously ignited, creating a hot combustion that would burn the house down? What if the fumes aggravated my migraines? Acrylics it was! They dried faster anyway.

After some time, I picked up a few charming old washboards and handsaws, and painted my beloved barns (and cows, turkeys, teepees, birds, trees, etc. etc.) on those, too. But where to store them? My husband, a roofer, was in the construction business and suggested a pegboard. This is a "perforated hardboard." Mine was a raw sienna color (I was developing a love of raw umber color and burnt sienna in particular) about eight feet wide and five or six feet tall, with holes all over its surface, and metal hooks that slid in wherever you wanted them. I set the pegboard against a wall in my front entrance hallway (for lack of any other available space to put it), and began to hang my finished blades there.

Word got around. A visitor to our house (we didn't have a steady stream of visitors, but we did get a few steady guests) had to pass right by the pegboard to get into the house. I had not planned it this way. In fact, I had never intended for anyone to really see my "work." But people did see it. My kids, my husband, my parents, my husband's family—they all began to talk about it and soon special orders were coming in. I was encouraged to show my blades at flea markets where they did extremely well. I would hand out a flyer I made myself on the computer with my contact info for special orders, and with a care sheet I'd written myself—one of the suggestions being not to display the painted saws outdoors, because they would rust even with the primer undercoat. Secretly, I hoped they all would rust and my paintings would disappear forever. I severely underpriced them, too. It was still a pastime and not really a serious undertaking. I was partaking in a fad craft and that's all it felt like.

I learned to keep nutritional foods nearby as I painted. I paced myself to balance chores and art, and I developed a routine of cleaning up my brushes and work area properly. I learned this the hard way after many of my favorite brushes hardened into unusable knobs and had to be discarded. I also learned that no matter how involved I was in rendering my landscapes (my mind would do the theta wave thing and be in a special calm place that I did not want to break free from), I simply *had* to use the toilet when I had the first urge. Another thing I did when I painted during those first few years of saws and painting, was to hold my breath. It was not conducive to enjoying the peace of mind I sought. I learned breathing control and even today I consistently remind myself about eating, bathroom importance, and not holding my breath. One thing I still find impossible to do while painting, is speaking. Perhaps this is part of my process and my speaking is with the paint out through my hands.

I did probably a thousand saw paintings then, and I know this because I kept a record book. I filled requests to paint a certain family-owned cabin named Camp Oregon. I even made a wooden model of their cabin to assist me, because I painted their cabin so much (I still have the wooden model to this day. It's made of wooden blocks and other found wooden pieces like Popsicle sticks, and painted over). I painted that cabin at least three times on various-sized round blades. I painted Camp Oregon scenes complete with deer and piled firewood on a couple of huge, six-feet-long, double-manned saws, too, which ended up hanging on the family's living room overhead beam.

There were other special orders—too many to name or even to remember as my record book is long gone now.

I painted a picture of a jockey on her horse and a special New Hampshire Inn painting, which was put on display in their lobby. I painted many subjects upon request: Indians, turkeys, deer, fish jumping out of a stream, you name it! This enabled me a little spending money for Christmas splurges or shoes for the children.

My three children are varied in temperaments, personalities, and disposition. My oldest is formally diagnosed with "high functioning" autism and selective mutism. As a child, he would take apart all our alarm clocks and gadgets and duct tape robotic parts to his action figures. But before doing so, he would line the parts up, studying what made a clock work, why the gears did what they did. Today he can fix and build computers. My middle son is a sensitive man, a compassionate and hard-working father who is, thus far, a nondriver like me. He, too, finds solace in art and I think it helps with his anxiety, which can seem overwhelming to him, I know. My daughter, the youngest, is a gifted artist, too, and has a knack for learning to play instruments. She has learned the guitar, cello, ukulele and violin. She, being transgender, is now my son, too, and lives as such.

When my oldest son reached high school, it became clear we needed a diagnosis for him at last. I was referred to an office in New Haven. The place smelled delightfully old, and smart. Lynn, his therapist, had met with my son several times and he underwent twenty hours of in-home evaluation. After his diagnosis, Lynn and I went through the same testing—this time for me.

My mother accompanied me when I went for my results. Lynn thought it best that I not know my IQ. She could mail it to me, but she said it was not a true indication of intelligence anyway, and I declined knowing. So there were peaks and valleys in my brain. I did learn from her that I scored above college level in writing, and comprehension of words, but there were so many blacks and whites. My math, for instance, was at fifth grade level . . .. That was not surprising! Wasn't it in fifth grade that I needed the damned tutor?

My mother was visibly shaking and stammering—smiling and laughing like she did when she was unnerved. She and the doctor, Lynn, sat near to each other, facing me, and I was alone to view them and the window, with its occasional pigeon fluttering by. Apparently I was "dysthymic," had a flat mood state. I was non-expressive, and as my mother confirmed, "She always was . . .." Her crepe paper eyelids were getting pink. I handed her a tissue box. I was elated. I was being explained! Lynn told her I fell somewhere along the autistic spectrum, specifically Asperger's. Smiling deep dimples into my plump cheeks, I told my mother it was not her fault that I never wanted any interaction with other kids.

I told her, "You had me in Brownies, Girl Scouts, camp; even became my leader. You had me take catechism with nuns, and you put me in the 4-H club, and even had me riding down Main Street waving to people in the annual Christmas parade. You brought me to your Dutchmaid, Artex, Tupperware, and food demonstration parties, where the man set the dessert on fire at the end! You sent me to go with Aunt Betty to watch her square dance, brought me to PTA meetings with you, and became the lunch lady at my school. You did all you could to 'socialize' me, and it hasn't failed. I'm just differently made-up. But it's normal, *for me.*"

Later, at home, I interrupted a baseball game on the TV to tell my husband I had Asperger's. Without hesitation, he replied in a melancholy tone, without ever turning away from the action on TV, "I always knew." I studied his face a long time. His features swirled and mixed up.

When I became pregnant in 1995 with my third child, my then daughter, my time became scarcer, and although I continued to immerse myself in art literature (I would many years later be told that I spoke as if I had a liberal arts education, which I probably did *give* myself through my studies), I put painting by the wayside. It had been a challenge. I had seen success and by this I mean I had learned something. Learning has always been my passion. When my daughter was three or four years old, I started trying my hand on canvas again, but just for something to do to pass the time and achieve that calm I so needed. Mostly though, I was writing. Writing a lot. I'd been selling my writing to small presses for six years at this point.

With the arrival of my mid-thirties and my youngest finally in school, there came a desire to get a formal education at last. My lifelong childhood friend—who had long ago shed her back brace, but now lived with MS—and I made the appointment to talk to an administrator at a local community college. I was nervous, but elated, too. My plans were changed by ALS, or Lou Gehrig's Disease. There would be no college for me. My husband was diagnosed with the disease. For the next five years, I chose to be his primary caregiver. No time for painting or for a personal indulgence like formal education.

But I kept learning through books and online sites, and I even found a unique way to reach that theta state through a new and original form of personal creative expression: miming! In my high-waisted black pants, striped shirt, and in full mime makeup, I fed him through his feeding tube or cleaned his many machines. I had mime modeling sessions with an RIT student. I ordered professional mime makeup online as my declining husband found solace in naps, remembering to adjust his body from time to time as I studied Marcel Marceau on the computer screen, or his paralyzed limbs would be in the same position I placed them in come morning. I never had my children or their friends finding it odd that I wore striped shirts, high-waisted pants, and suspenders. My mimed face wasn't odd because they were used to my eccentricities. Miming as I went about chores allowed me a creative release and it was a coping mechanism, too—an outlet . . . while he died slowly in front of my white face, with black diamonds painted over my eyebrows. Mimes did not have to speak.

My next painting "first" came about in 2005. I was newly widowed with three children and found support through The Connecticut Autism Pilot Project. When Alison came to my house to interview me and acquaint me with the program and how it could help me, she asked if I had any special talents. Of course, by this time, I had a book written and was seeking a publisher, and so I mentioned that.

She wrote this down and then asked, "Anything else?"

"Well," I said hesitantly, "I used to paint a lot . . .."

She asked to see some paintings and I hesitated again. But I went to my closet and pulled out the half-hearted canvases. As Alison looked through them, I noticed something. It was a shine in her eyes, a flicker in her eyebrows: they kind of twitched up like inch worms.

"You can do something with this," she said. And I had absolutely *zero* idea what she meant by that.

Within a few months, Alison and my assigned "friend" and helper, Barb, had arranged a "first" for me and a handful of other autistic artists in the program: *a gallery showing in New Haven!* Unlike me, the other autistic artists did not have SM in addition to their autism. When it came time to do a Q&A with the gathered crowd at the art show, I did my best. I was not good-natured like my peers; at ease and fluid in my speech, but my voice did **not** disappear. I was proud. Myself and another artist were interviewed about art when Keri Bowers came to town. We all had dinner in Hartford, with Keri and her son. Then we went to the gallery where our art was hung, and we talked about art. I was in Keri's documentary style film called *ARTS*.

Other firsts were in store for me that year. I sold a few paintings at that New Haven showing with my peers—the first paintings on canvas I'd ever sold. Walking the arts district in New Haven with Barb, sitting in artsy cafes with bathroom murals in them, going to museums, sculpture displays, and into bead shops. All firsts. All wonderful! I was encouraged to put a winter scene of mine on Christmas cards, which sold well. I sold many professionally produced prints of this scene as well. Still, I was not completely happy with my sense of color choices, contrast, and hues. I was still learning.

Barb got me a paying mural job in a day center for disabled adults. It wasn't the first mural I'd participated in creating, but it was *my* first mural. I painted two walls. The subjects I chose were mine: a barn, of course, a young man doing a wheelie in his wheelchair, birds on a fence, a hot air balloon, a small lake with ducks . . . I even put Barb in the painting.

"Shave off a few pounds when you paint me, please!" she said.

"Nope. I can't do that," I said. "It would not be you if I did that."

I ended up leaving the program after a whirlwind few years of much-needed support, job coaching, social skills group, and, of course, friendship with Barb, which I cherished. I even made a friend from the group named Rich. A first indeed! We got together a few times outside the program and chatted on the phone sometimes.

"I hate to quit," I said to Alison. But I had a new fiancé who lived with me, was helping with my kids, and I could not easily divide my time.

"Don't think of it as quitting," said Alison. "Think of it as graduating."

I continued to paint on canvas every chance I got. I submitted to agents and publishers, and soon I was holding my own memoir in my hands. All on my own, I began realizing I could set up gallery shows for myself. I was showing in a few shows a year and selling paintings in nearly every show. Could I write, or even paint, my way out of public housing? I doubted this, so I enjoyed the process wherever it took me. The important thing is, I didn't wait for someone to see my work. I put my work out there to see. For someone who could barely tolerate parting with my paintings (as I said in Keri's docufilm), I was now actively developing a market for it. I subconsciously realized if art was my voice, then if no one sees it, they don't "hear" that voice.

I began submitting my art to online selling sites, such as KindTree and Vango, and sold note cards and paintings that way. I submitted to authors seeking artwork for art books, and imagine my surprise when Debra Hosseini, author of *The Art of Autism*, notified me that my "Shattered Image" piece, a self portrait of myself looking down into a broken mirror, was selected for the cover of the book. The theme was "shattering the myths of autism," and so my painting fit the theme.

Since my "Shattered Image" painting (acrylic on paper) had been sold the year before to a special education teacher for his office (I didn't even remember his name!), I wasn't sure if the one picture I had taken of this painting was saved in high resolution quality in the right format to be on the cover of a book. This is when I realized the importance of owning a high quality camera. I had to learn this the hard way, too. The final *Art of Autism* book, with my painting on the cover, is just beautiful, but Debra had to use a likeness much smaller than intended because of the poor photo quality and the pixilation that occurred if it was enlarged too much. I researched how to catalog *all* my art in quality photographs (taken by me), because after paintings were sold, I continued to submit the photos of my sold paintings to "Calls for Submissions."

I ended up having my art reproduced in *Been There. Done That. Try This!* (Attwood), and many other books. There was one particular call for writing submissions that I answered from Carl Sutton, and this ended up being a first I'm especially proud of. I ended up writing several heartfelt essays for his and Cheryl's book, *Selective Mutism In Our Own Words*. In fact, my fiancé Al bought me a Corel digital art program for my computer and I designed the cover for Carl's book. On the cover of the book is a digital rendering of me that I designed—me at the age of about eight, with tape over my mouth to symbolize mutism. I guess I'm the poster child for SM now, right? Actually, this book was the first time I ever really talked in a raw and honest way about selective mutism. I'd always been honest about Asperger's, especially in my memoir, but this book still seems like the most important thing I've ever been a part of. I'm proud of my memoir, proud of my accomplishments so far, but this SM book has the power to teach so many people who are silenced that they too can have a voice.

For me, I was beginning to realize, consciously now, that although my vocal cords were often silenced, my art was loud and speaking for me. And that is how it has always been. I had never truly been more aware of this until this moment. Which brings me to my latest "first," one I am very honored to have been a part of.

As an author and artist, I taught myself web design and created a website. I learned to blog and created my own outlet for words and thoughts and ideas. I used Twitter, LinkedIn, and Facebook to discuss art with peers, and to meet new contacts in the arenas of my passions: writing, arts, autism, advocacy, and SM.

One of the contacts who "friended" me on my Facebook author page happened to be Elizabeth Stringer Keefe, a professor at Lesley College, Cambridge. I loved the cityscape and history that is the Boston area—so close, yet so far from my Valley life. It was 2015 when she messaged me about a 2016 show, and I'd had regular art showings with AANE, so I knew the area a little. One of the shows through AANE had been in Boston. Thankfully, Al could be my driver.

Elizabeth asked me to be a part of the *3+ Artists: Celebrating Autism* show she was planning. She not only wanted me to show my work in their gallery at the college with two other autistic artists, but she wanted me to do a "presentation" and have a book signing. I said "Yes" immediately, and be damned the consequences of what I was getting myself into! I told myself I could do this. My inner voice wanted me to do this and I trusted that voice.

Because Elizabeth read my memoir, she was aware that speaking in front of a crowd was something I may not be able to do.

"We'll work this out," she assured me. "It's going to be so fun. We'll accommodate whatever you need to make this work."

That's all I needed to hear. I accepted that for me (unlike my two peers in the show, who I greatly respected and admired), speaking in front of an audience was not something that was going to happen. SM is a cruel affliction. *But it's okay*, I told myself, *to sometimes accept special accommodations, to accept help*. For the months leading up to the big event, I painted my heart out on canvas, framing until sometimes 2 a.m. But if I thought *I* was working hard, Elizabeth was doing all of the preparations for an entire show, along with help, of course, but she was behind the scenes and juggling lots of tasks. She emailed me once that trying to set up the show and all its presentations was like "building a sand castle and every time it seemed built, the waves would come and wash a little of it away" and she'd have to start again.

When I arrived at the show, I met Stephen Shore, a person who is widely known in the autism world. He was a speaker. I was very disappointed I could not seem to speak to him. He was a peer I respected. I wanted to discuss many autism issues and couldn't. I was a walking nerve and I hoped I would not appear to be giving him a rude, cold shoulder. It was not a good start, but I refused to let dread creep in and sabotage this opportunity.

I did, however, manage to talk about my artwork one on one with patrons. I also held a book signing and sold every book I brought. Although I'd signed books before, this was my *first* real signing event, and I was thrilled I could speak fluently one on one with buyers. Finally, it was time for *my* presentation.

"The voice is gone," I mouthed to Elizabeth.

She called for a brief intermission before it was time for my talk, and during this time she came up with a brilliant accommodation for me. We positioned me in a chair in front of the audience, turned to the side to block out most of the sensory stimuli of the audience—the very thing taking away my speech. Elizabeth put her laptop on my lap, hooked it to an overhead screen that the audience could see, and gave me a quick tutorial on how to use the laptop. I put on my glasses and studied the keyboard as the audience filed in and took their seats. Many of them were holding my memoir. After Elizabeth introduced me, I typed onto the keyboard and the screen filled with my words. I was communicating. *My* way! And that was okay. The first thing I did was to type an apology for not facing them. I explained my challenges and then Elizabeth, with a nod from me, began to read passages from my book that we had chosen beforehand.

I was told later that my fiancé Al, who was in the first row, was nearly in tears, and Elizabeth stumbled a little, due to strong emotions that *my* written words were evoking in her. Powerful emotions are so hard to regulate for me. And here were my words coming out of Elizabeth's mouth. My thoughts typed onto a screen.

After Elizabeth would read a passage, she'd pause and it was my turn to type. The place was quiet except for my typing. I'd give my impressions, my backstory, my thought processes behind the passage that Elizabeth had read. She read about twenty passages and each time she paused, I would add my thoughts, which appeared on the screen. Sometimes I'd be funny, and I'd hear people laughing around and behind me, from the audience. Laughing *with* me, not *at* me, mind you, and that's important to note.

After the show, I sold seven or eight paintings. But here's the first, the first that trumps all my firsts: I had done something very outside my comfort zone and it had been a success, not because I sold paintings and books, but because I effectively communicated. Having a celebration dinner downstairs with Al after the show, I was beaming. I couldn't stop smiling. The steak was lousy actually, but my confidence was soaring. In fact, I was invited back to Lesley College for a show in April 2017 to "speak" at a symposium for gifted children. I said "Yes," of course, and damn my preconceived comfort zone. I know I can push that.

Elizabeth was willing to accommodate me in a much-appreciated way. I respect her for that. During my dinner, I got to thinking about all the work she put in to make that show happen. What a beautiful thing to do. I got to thinking about her metaphor. About how all her work to pull it off felt like waves washing away a carefully built castle on the beach.

After I had my celebratory dinner, it was time to head home. I lived in Connecticut—several hours from Boston. I had to miss the "meet and greet" in the gallery and I was perfectly okay with that! I went up to Elizabeth to thank her before I left.

"It went so well," I said. "I'd say the flag is on top of the castle right about now."

She looked confused.

"The sand castle," I said. "The flag's on top."

When she understood my word play, she smiled and asked if she could hug me. I don't grant that sort of thing to just anyone, because hugs feel like indents afterward, which can't be popped back out for hours at times. But we hugged, or I sort of patted her, which is my hug, and I thanked her.

I went to see Elizabeth again when I picked up some unsold paintings. I brought her morning glories I had grown from seeds, because I imagined them entwining themselves colorfully, all over her porch rail. Somewhere. Wherever she called home. And maybe they'd remind her of me and how thankful I was to have been given a chance to succeed on terms that met my needs. I didn't know—had no way of knowing—that they were her favorite flowers.

How many more firsts await me?

What's the next presentation at Lesley College going to be like?

I'm working on several fiction essays and a second memoir. Maybe it'll be a bestseller and that'd be a first, because it means I'd be *communicating* to a larger crowd. Really, any successes I've had began with support from other people. With their words, I replaced mantras in my head (like: are you deaf, dumb, or stupid?) with the following:

My late husband's remark at the flea market: "We'll buy you some blades, then."

And Alison: "You can do something with this."

And Al: "I'll be by your side and support you the whole way."

These remarks eventually became a presentation at a college in a city I love! It wasn't the first lousy steak I've ever eaten, but it was my first celebratory dinner and the steak doesn't diminish how I felt.

Back when I was little, and used to be mesmerized by the little pot with the rattling vent hole, I asked my mother, "What happens if the vent hole is not there? If the steam can't get out?"

She answered me with a story about the time she was babysitting and decided to make the kids some food in a pressure cooker. She had no idea how to use one, hadn't researched this at all or asked for any help beforehand. In fact, she used it incorrectly. Someone could've seriously been hurt. The lid ended up building up so much pressure, it blew off and hit the ceiling!

Art is my rattling vent hole. It provides an escape. A much needed cleansing, and a way to let the unexpressed be expressed. I'd hate to think of my life without it. I'll bet that day in Cambridge at the college, just like the glint I saw in Alison's eyes, I shone. I'll have more firsts . . . but these I share here with you humble me and I cherish them. Beyond mere words.

Heart in a Bottle
Christina Pires

As a young woman with autism, I was not entirely sure when I would actually experience love. No, it's not because I don't believe in it: I am in love with love—a romantic in every sense of the word. And it's not because I can't feel it either, but rather because I wanted to take my time with it. I went through my late teens and early- to mid-twenties focused on school and nothing else. Close friends and relatives hinted I should enjoy dating, too. "You're only getting *older!*" they'd say. I insisted that when the time, and most importantly *the person* were right, I would know. Everything would naturally fall into place, and I preferred it that way. In truth, part of my secret reasoning was I wasn't sure if a man would be interested in the challenge of being involved with me.

I am a quirky individual; I do odd things. For example, when I am happy or genuinely excited over something, I find myself clapping—something I have done since I was a child, it's on home video. When I am under intense emotional or psychological stress, I do the classic hand-flapping motion, pacing back and forth, not wanting to be embraced or touched until I'm calm again and initiate it. I'm also prone to walking on my tip-toes at random, and obsessing over things that most people would agree should not matter so much to me, but I can't help it.

There are a lot of things that people automatically think are true regarding people with autism. One of the biggest, grossly incorrect assumptions is the belief that we're unemotional creatures; that we do not feel anything (love, fear, hate, empathy); and that these are foreign concepts we can't comprehend or reciprocate.

That is terribly offensive: I am a *human being* with a heart and a brain, so *of course* I am going to have feelings and understand others do, too. I think that plays a big part in the belief that we can't be in relationships or have families, because they don't think we know how that works, or that we can't be serious enough for it. But that couldn't be further from the truth, either. I ache and yearn for companionship and love just as any *normal* person would. Just because I am quirky doesn't mean I don't want those things.

Another annoying assumption is that people think I hate going out and doing things, hate being social, or hate people in general. While socializing even with just one person is exhausting for me, I don't *hate* any of those! I enjoy going out with a few close friends—in as small a group as possible—and having a good time. The chief reason I don't go out often can be summed up in two words: sensory overload. When the background noise gets loud I go into a panic, and can't focus at all on the people I'm with. It takes a lot of effort to stay focused, and not run for the nearest door. So, as long as I'm with the right people, I can handle it a bit better.

I'm extremely shy and awkward when meeting new people for the first time, wanting to disappear into a corner rather than socialize. All I can think of is how nice and quiet my room is, how comforting my pajamas are, and how I can't wait to get into them again. Usually, though, as long as someone is with me, I get just a touch more comfortable and begin talking.

I am often identified as "quirky," "odd," or—and this is my favorite—"eccentric" when I come into contact with new people for the first time, and that's because of one simple fact: this form of autism is invisible to others around me. For example, my cousin Ivan, a school psychologist for the L.A. Unified School District, noticed I was a bit different behavioral wise when he first met me, but couldn't identify what made me stand out, because we'd only spend a few minutes together between classes. The more time I spent around him, the more traits he began to recognize, and by the time my mother told him I had autism, he went, "Ah! Okay, got it now: everything makes sense." What did he mean by that, exactly? He was referring to how I act: the tense body language, the awkwardness of socializing, and the withdrawn shyness—that's what everyone sees first.

If they are able to last around me long enough without going insane or getting frustrated, they begin to notice other things. They see I get stuck on obsessive loops, fixated on a person, place, or thing: I could be talking Darth Vader one week, and suddenly it's Heath Ledger's Joker the next. What's commonly mistaken for forgetfulness is due to not being able to retain information past a certain point. If I am asked to do five steps, I will remember the first two and go into a blank panic on the rest. Repetition helps, but I still sometimes forget some steps.

Luckily, though, I have people in my corner who are very supportive, loving, and understanding of the autism. Most of the family embraces and accepts it, especially since it's been confirmed that one of my younger cousins has Asperger's. They've learned that we Aspie girls are different, but it's the *being different* that makes us unique. There's at least one family member whom I now know made fun of me while I was growing up, and was very much a jerk about it from what I have been told, but luckily those who care outnumber him. My aunt Lydia is one such person; she helped Mom in the early years of raising me, is so very patient, and has always found my OCD patterns to be fun and interesting.

Mom, of course, is proud as a peacock if we're getting into a game of similes about it. She was nervous in the beginning of course, or rather suspicious when she noticed I was a bit *off* compared to other children she had watched grow up. The diagnosis was overwhelming for her, especially as a single mother, but she never shied away from me. If anything, it made her stronger, and she instilled that strength in me. She told me and still tells me that I can *do* anything, and *be* anything that I desire to be. She also strived to teach me that someone *will* love me, and that a real man will take me as I am—quirks and all.

While I love my family and my friends, there are certain things I keep to myself. For instance, I have never told any of them I avoided dating because I had no idea how I would ever connect deep enough with someone to enter a serious courtship; the very idea of it was stressful. I sometimes frustrate people, as I frustrate myself with my quirks on a bad day. There have even been times when I questioned myself as to who was going to want to have that in their life, or, more specifically, to have *me*. Honestly, I was secretly terrified there wasn't anyone in the world I could match with.

However, life is a rather funny thing; it throws you curve balls when you aren't even looking to catch anything, and the summer of 2015 was when the curve ball hit me head-on. I was on YouTube at the time, listening to *Youth of America* by Birdbrain, as I had just finished watching *Scream* for the two hundredth time. (I automatically hunt down the soundtrack after a movie fires me up—it's just a need that I always have had.) While I was there, I entered a previous conversation thread with one of the posters. I later learned his name was Kirk. We chatted back and forth for a while, almost a year of silence went by, and then in October of 2016, we resumed our conversation—*and didn't stop.* He and I quickly hit it off, carrying over to Facebook, which was unexpected and thrilling for me all at once. The scariest thing was when we decided to try video chatting; that meant seeing each other for the first time. I was nervous and excited; I could feel my palms getting sweaty and my heart pounding when I tapped that green phone button and waited for him to pick up.

For once, I was not deceived regarding appearances— he looked just like his picture on Facebook. Short, neatly cropped, dark-brown hair dipped and weaved in and out of itself in slight curls on top of his head. His eyes looked darker in the light of his room, but I remembered from his profile photo that they were a piercing, pale blue. His skin tone was fair, he was clean-shaven, and, thankfully, not terribly tall— five foot three. He was dressed very comfy casual like I was, sporting a blue t-shirt (I think it was blue), and I want to say either jeans or sweats, I can't remember for sure.

His smile was so terribly warm and inviting, as was his personality, which was extremely colorful, free, and boisterous like my own. I had only ever been exposed to an Irish accent through film, but hearing an Irish native speak the way he did was such a fun experience. His accent wasn't overly thick or hard to understand, and I enjoyed hearing him talk, as I had never known anyone from that part of the U.K. What did that sound like, exactly? Here are the best examples: I was given many nicknames, as according to him, in Ireland, people addressed each other by those, so I got used to the way he said certain words. Pet sounded like "peht," love sounded like "luhv," and Chrissy—the one nickname I swore up and down was far too uppity and girlish for me to *ever* consider using—sounded like "Chriseh."

I don't like lying to people—I find it so terribly rude and wrong—and so I made sure not to misrepresent myself to him, either. I feel rather bashful describing myself, but here it goes. I'm small statured, standing at five feet, zero inches in height, affording me just enough inches to make it onto rollercoasters. My hair was once a blondish color, but has since darkened with age to brunette, sitting just past my shoulders and growing. I have a round-shaped face with a "button" nose and hazel "moon" eyes, as those who have met me call them; they're not huge, but they are sort of big I guess.

I look like my mom, who, in turn, looks like her mom—that's the Pires line, all of the women in the family look alike. Mom's a fiery woman in her fifties with shoulder-length, golden-brown hair, brown eyes, and a loud, lively laugh. She's also a true Portuguese native, an islander. She was born in Portugal in a chain of islands known as the Azores. She told me my great great uncle sponsored her father so he and his family could come over to America to settle. And so they crossed the North Atlantic in a huge cargo plane, and began a new chapter in Bakersfield, California, in March of 1961.

Now, Mom is protective, given I am her only child and I have autism, so she's used to jumping in as my advocate. When it came to me being involved seriously with someone, she told me she would always be there for advice. She has only ever wanted me to be happy no matter whom I choose to be with. She advised to just use my best judgment, and, if that didn't work, I could come to her for help.

Little were either of us aware just how deep of a connection I was making with Kirk. The more we wrote each other, the more I came to realize my feelings were beyond friendship for him. I knew I'd have to confess that I loved him; if I didn't act fast enough, some other lucky girl would come along and sweep him up and away. However, before I decided to drop the L-word, I knew I had to do my "main confession" first: I had to tell him about the autism. His reaction would tell me if the "I love you" should follow.

We were still feeling each other out in November when I casually slipped that I had autism into the conversation. I'd never felt so sick waiting for a response before. Not even a minute later, he typed back that he knew exactly what Asperger's was—a relative's son had it as well, so he understood the quirks, repetitious behaviors, and obsessive patterns. The wave of relief was overwhelming; it felt like I had somehow materialized all of my hopes and dreams of the person I'd want to fall in love with into flesh and blood.

The next thing I knew, we had confessed we loved each other, and began dating in January 2017.

As he lived in Ireland and I in California, timing our online chats was somewhat tricky, but we made it work. Time and distance meant nothing to us: we were in love and those things were, to quote Brandon Lee in *The Crow*, "trivial." Mom would come out to the living room to say "Hello," but tried staying in her room to give us our privacy. Around February, as I sat on the other end of the couch, Mom was in the living room chatting with Kirk, and asked if I had mentioned the autism to him. There was a slight pause, and then I heard him respond enthusiastically, unintimidated or afraid, "Oh aye, she did, and honestly that doesn't bother me at all." Another wave of relief; my heart even skipped a beat— this relationship was *perfect* . . . or so I thought.

We had been together for the better part of three months when I had to make the most nerve-wracking video chat to date. We were pretty serious—I mean, we never talked about marriage, more like skirted past it in a flurry of shyness. I now know that when I would leave the room, he had hinted several times to Mom that he wanted to give me a ring. I, in turn, had hinted several times that if he ever asked me I would say, "Yes." That is how much he meant to me, that is how much I loved him, and that is what made the idea of approaching him on the subject of drinking too much so damn scary.

I was so very confused the entire length of that weekend from hell in March.

How did it get to this point, and how did something so major fly right on past me? I should have been able to see this a mile away: I grew up with an alcoholic—my biological father. I remember how difficult that was, how intimidating, loud, and angry he would be when he'd been drinking. He would yell at Mom, he would yell at *me* when I would come on the court-sanctioned visits on weekends, he would throw things, and kick holes into doors. More times than not, I was afraid of him, because I had no idea what would set him off, and I would sometimes unintentionally get him upset. For example, one night his unnecessary angered reaction came from a question I asked while he helped me clean up my room: was David Bowie's hair in *Labyrinth* real or a wig?

When he officially left us in 1998, I wasn't sad at all, but extremely overjoyed. It was like watching the Wicked Witch melt in *The Wizard of Oz*: a quick movement of his shadow on the ceiling of my bedroom, and he was gone. For the first time, I felt pure *relief*—I knew the nightmare was over.

Growing up, I did consider my future several times, particularly when it came to serious relationships, love, and one day hopefully being married. I swore to myself I would never end up with a man like my father. I had lived through that pain, disappointment, and fear once; I refused to do it again.

It's true, my Irish beau liked to venture out to the pub. He told me it was an activity he enjoyed doing frequently. Okay, so he liked to go out and have a good time and there's nothing wrong with that, right? There is if the man's calling you intoxicated, but I'd dismissed it the past two instances. I know what you're thinking: I said I grew up with an alcoholic, so why did this guy get a pass? Honestly, I wasn't really paying attention—this was my first serious relationship, my first real brush with love, so I was completely unprepared, and it snuck up on me. I won't deny it; it's true that I had seen him drunk a number of times at this point.

The first time was New Year's Eve: that was acceptable; we had both been drinking, no big deal. The second time was in early March around the time of his birthday: alright that was unexpected, but again, I brushed it off easily. The worry began when Mom pointed out there was a pattern that had slowly developed over the course of our relationship. When I first started talking to him he was always sober, I never ever saw him drunk until New Year's Eve. The worst of the drunken calls was the most recent: St. Patrick's Day weekend. That means in Ireland it's not just one day of celebration, but *three,* he told me.

I may be new to dating, but I am not stupid; I understood perfectly he had friends and interests prior to meeting me. I am not a demanding girlfriend; I didn't expect him to be glued to his phone (essentially to me) while he was out having fun. So, while it was a bit startling to hear that, I wasn't bothered he'd be away. Besides, I was made aware a few weeks earlier this was just something he traditionally did every year.

He said I would most likely hear from him on Saturday, as he was going to an event on Friday with some friends. No problem, I said, go have fun, but be safe. Saturday morning came; I left my usual greeting saying I hoped he slept well and had fun out and about. That's where the first sign popped up that something was terribly wrong. I didn't hear back from him that morning, which was very odd.

Normally, by 9 a.m. my time, I would receive a morning response from him. We had been doing this for the past three months; it was almost like a natural reflex at that point. I would type, wait a few minutes, soak in some coffee, and boom: he would respond back while I was at my desk. It was completely out of character for him, but I wasn't too worried. He had been out celebrating, so perhaps he was still asleep in bed having got in not too long ago his time. So, I proceeded to wait.

Morning turned into afternoon, afternoon slowly dissolved into evening, and still there was no word from him. I was beside myself with worry at that point: I had no way to get in touch with him. I couldn't even reach out to his mother to ask if he was okay, because I had never met her, and from what I was told, she was in and out of the house. I am not the sort of person who usually goes to the "what if" questions, but that day I couldn't get them to shut up—they just kept pouring out, covering my brain in worrisome goo. All I kept hearing was, *What if he got into an accident somewhere and can't call for help? What if he's hurt?* **What if he's dead?**

Around 11 p.m. California time, I decided to check my phone one last time as I felt rather horrible physically; I remember hurting everywhere. There was a missed video chat on Messenger. I went back to my room to call him back; he did not pick up. I opened Messenger on my laptop and began hurriedly typing, "I saw I missed your call. Are you okay? Are you there?" It looked like he was trying to type back, but the pattern seemed sporadic, so I typed, "Did you make it back home alright? Are you home now?" It was very quiet for several minutes, and then the notification came that he was trying to video chat me again, so this time I answered.

What I heard from the other end sounded like a person in the middle of a stroke or seizure. I didn't actually see him at first; I could only make out unintelligible sounds through the speaker. I turned to find Mom standing in the doorway to my room completely taken aback by the noises.

She came closer to my desk, all five foot three of her towered over me as I sat dumbfounded in my chair, mouth agape, and phone in hand producing inhuman noises. Frowning, she nodded to the phone and asked, "What *is* that?" I was very hesitant to answer her, but she and I both knew what the noise was. After pausing and swallowing slightly, I told her reluctantly, "He called me back, but I can't understand him." I looked back over to her for guidance in a sheer, helpless panic. Now, I struggle with reading people, but in that moment I could clearly read her face and it said one word in mom language: *unacceptable.* She told me I need to end the call, to tell him I will talk tomorrow, and then quietly left the room. I turned my attention back to my cellphone screen: he was finally in the frame, but could barely sit up in his chair.

He was so badly uncoordinated that he fell face-first onto his desk where his head made a loud, smacking sound. As he gradually tried to lift himself up into a sitting position, still attempting very hard to speak to me, I tried to talk over all of the sounds he was making. "Babe," I said trying to catch his attention, "you need to go to bed. I can't talk to you right now—I can barely understand anything you're saying." Talking to him in that state, I had flashbacks of my father: all of that nervous energy came back up from a dark, repressed, padlocked corner of my psyche. I felt myself grow tense; my arms and legs shook. He finally got into his chair, though he was very unsteadily sitting at that point, as he continued to try and talk over me.

Calm, commanding, serious, and quiet: I repeated those words in my head trying to maintain focus to remove myself from the situation. I said to him again, "You need to go to bed, I cannot talk to you, you're not making sense, and so I will contact you tomorrow." Call it a sign or whatever it is that works for you, but at that precise moment, the video call lost its connection and dropped. I went back to the laptop and typed one final message, "Go to bed. We'll talk tomorrow ♥." I then contacted one of my cousins, stating, "I need your help: I think he has a problem, and I don't know how to approach him about it."

Our relationship was an open and trusting one: we pretty much talked about anything and everything with each other. We weren't shy, by any means, about discussing serious subjects, such as kids, where we wanted to go career-wise, our health worries, and things like that. "Never be afraid to talk to me about things, Love. You can tell me anything, Chrissy." He had said this repeatedly, but that didn't make my telling him I think he drank too much any easier. It was an extremely difficult thing to say, much like it was when I had once approached my father on the subject. I was stuck in place for such a long time on how to even begin the conversation when I saw him again.

My cousin suggested writing a short comment card or telephone script, with specific cues to touch on, so I would not lose my train of thought or become so emotional that I couldn't get it out. I usually use the script concept when I have to make important calls: this definitely qualified. I was on edge as soon as I woke up on March 19, 2017, and counting down to the hour when I would call him never felt so forced or out of place as it did then. I hadn't even spoken to him yet, and already I felt this suffocating, panicked feeling. Those terrible "what if" questions came back to kill me.

What if you didn't pick the right words to say to him?
What if you start to cry in the middle of saying everything?
What if he gets mad and this escalates into a nasty fight?
What if he tells you that it's over?
What are you going to do, Tina?
What are you going to do?

When I finally tapped the video chat symbol on my phone, I was shaking. I felt so nervous I could feel bile and acid burning in the pit of my stomach; I wanted to abort. I wanted to go back to when we'd exchanged the "I love you" on New Year's Eve. I wanted to find out where it was that everything had gone so far off track. Which hidden social cue had I missed? He wasn't like this at the start, never called while intoxicated like that, and it only seemed to get worse each time he did it. And that's when the word finally hit me, the one I'd been searching for: *comfortability*. He had become so comfortable around me now that he had let the mask slip down a bit—a mask he wasn't even aware he'd been wearing, judging by what happened as I spoke with him.

He was smiling, quite cheerful and eager to chat as always when I saw him. I wasn't smiling like I usually did when I saw him fade onto my screen, not that day. I kept my expression blank, my tone serious and calm, as I told him he had scared me to death. I had no idea if something had happened to him, I said, no way of finding out if he was hurt, because he never contacted me like he had promised he would. He nodded; he told me he could explain it to me so I could understand it better. There were a few things that had happened over the weekend, which really screwed up his plans.

He said a good friend of his had told him there was something going on at a pub on Friday night when he was going out. He waited for quite a while at the venue only to discover nothing was happening there like he was told, so he went home upset. "So you made it home. Why didn't you just let me know that?" I asked. The answer was unbelievable: "I didn't contact you because I didn't want to be a bother."

*You left me worried sick because you didn't want to be a bother. You have **got** to be kidding.*

I felt like I was quiet for a very, very long time as I stared into my cellphone at him. I slowly asked why in the world he would think sending a simple message assuring me he was safe would be a bother to me. I loved him I told him; naturally, I was going to be worried when he didn't respond to me the entire day. He then admitted, in between being frustrated, he was drinking at home that night, too. He knew he tended to be a bit much for everyone around him to handle when he was drunk he told me.

"Yeah, I know," I said, "because you called me late last night."

He frowned, shaking his head with his voice soft and confused as he said, "I...I *didn't* call you." "Yes, you did— *twice*," I told him as he sat there still frowning at me and shaking his head. "It was bad," I told him. "You were making sounds instead of words. You sounded like you were either stroking or seizing, and you could barely sit up in your chair. You actually fell out of it a few times, and you hit your head, too. You kept slamming it down because you couldn't sit up." He remained dumbfounded looking as if I had described something that never happened, which I came to quickly realize meant the worst drunk type of all: the blackout.

It's hard to truly describe how I felt that day or even at that exact moment, as it was a mixture of things. I felt wedged between frustration and extreme worry for him. I was frustrated he didn't get back to me when he said he would, knowing I was waiting for an answer to know he was alright. His additional answer to that was he had been "too drunk to type."

I took a breath, and brought up my Word document with his name on it as I talked to him. I do not have the original wording I used, having deleted the document months ago. It felt horrible having it on my desktop, so I was only too happy to toss it when I was done. Below is a short version—with some of the wording I remember using when I talked to him. I still remember shaking; I could feel my eyes get prickly at times, and it felt like there was a lump in my throat. However, I spoke calmly and steadily to him as I read from my prompt carefully.

"Listen: I really need to talk to you about something that's very important. You told me I should never be afraid to talk to you about things, and this is something I need to get out there, because it has me concerned. I think you have a problem; the reason I am saying this is because I grew up with an alcoholic father, and I saw what it did to him. I am not saying this because I'm trying to be a nag, and I don't want you thinking I'm trying to be a controlling bitch of a girlfriend or anything like that. I'm saying all of this because *I love you*, and I am very worried about you."

It was like addressing my father, Brian, all over again, in his garage, on a hot summer afternoon, just before going back home to Mom. I had done this all before, felt myself shaking, and felt the same fear and intimidation while Brian walked around smoking and drinking. I'm not even sure how I got onto the subject or idea to try and change him for the better. I was still in high school I think, and still trying so very hard to make Brian a part of my life. That was despite his being absent for the whole thing, even the years when he had been physically there.

I remember I had half-heartedly teased my absentee dad about getting him to quit smoking, to which he replied, "No." I then pointed to the tall, silver beer can in his hand. "How about that?" I had asked him, and then added, "I'm serious." I couldn't tell you what else I had said to him, it's been way too long now, but I do remember bursting into tears that I didn't know were coming.

Brian had hugged me, mumbled something about trying I think, I can't exactly remember. It didn't matter; he never did try, not even after I begged him that day. I did not care for how history was repeating itself with my boyfriend, this young man I wanted to spend the rest of life with. No, I would not let it win, not again: I would be completely truthful about my feelings and honest with Kirk, just like he told me I could be and we'd work through it.

My boyfriend patted at the air as if trying to ease my fears, or possibly calm down a woman in hysterics. He shook his head looking at me as he said, "Oh, no, Pet. Listen, I am not an alcoholic." I nodded, but I could still feel myself shaking as I waited patiently for him to explain further. He went on for a bit, letting me know he didn't normally get that drunk, that this was just a one-time event. He promised he would not call me drunk ever again, and also said he would make sure to let me know when he had made it back home safely after going out so I would not worry.

Great; so, problem solved and relationship strain successfully avoided, right? I really want to tell you, "Yes." You have no idea just how much I wish I could say that. If I say that, it means we jumped the hurdle together. It also means I am one step closer to possibly getting one thing I crave from life. Sadly, from here the relationship took a drastic turn for the worst.

The afternoon didn't get any better as I had more bad news to give him. As I was/am only a student, it was going to be impossible for me to fly to Ireland. I felt so guilty and terrible for having to say it, but it was something he needed to be aware of, as it was a rather big problem. What he said next threw me even further than his comment about being bothersome had.

"Listen," he said to me in a very quiet, serious tone, while I stood pacing back and forth in my room, phone in hand, "if you don't think this is working out, you can feel free to call it. Me? I'm happy. I don't have any problems with the distance or anything like that. But if it's not working for you, that's okay." In that moment, I could feel my stomach drop clear down past my knees.

It was like he took out a knife, sunk it as deep as it could go through my heart, and slowly started twisting it. I felt so sick and panicked; I could feel myself heading into an emotional spiral. No, no, no—I did not want to lose this. He was *perfect*: I *loved* him, we completed each other, and we were *the same*. I had never found sameness, understanding, or love until I met him. I would not let him go, because I could not let him go; it simply was not an option for me.

I remember being very quiet, going back and forth in circles near the entryway to my room. I think he'd gone to get water or use the restroom, I don't remember, but I had gone back to my mother. She had been nearby the whole time in our kitchen, washing dishes *and* listening in just in case the call turned into a verbally violent one. I held the phone to my chest and had approached her quietly repeating the horrible words he had said to me. I had whispered in disbelief, "He said if I wanted to break up, he was fine with it. He is leaving it up to me."

Mom was quiet before leaning forward and looking at me saying, "Then it is your decision; whatever *you* want to do." Looking back on it now, I know she was infuriated with him. He was taking the easy way out of this, because the truth was he hadn't liked what I'd said and wasn't interested anymore.

Then it happened: I went from panic and fear into a state of numbness as I went back to my bedroom. I re-approached him again, letting everything I felt give him my answer. "I don't want to end this. I love you so very much. I can't let us go. I think we are doing okay, that we can keep going forward like we want to. You've become part of my daily rituals, my life—I don't want to let that go."

*I can't let that go—I'm not that kind of a girlfriend, I am **not** giving up on us.*

He made one request: to speak with my mother as I had told him she was incredibly upset with him. He didn't want any bad blood or feelings between them, he told me, and so I reluctantly asked Mom if she could speak to him. I left the two of them alone, but I could still hear Mom's quiet tone—the scary one she used when she was angry. After all was said and I hung up with him, Mom told me she gave him a warning, which she was passing onto me. "You may be a grown woman, but I am telling you right now that if I catch him calling you drunk like that ever again, I will come in and disconnect the call."

Filled with guilt and unable to rest, Kirk had called me back again later that night. He wanted very much to talk to my mother, where he profusely tried to stop any bleeding in their relationship. When he went to bed, I felt hopeful—the fact that he called again meant he did understand what I had said, and wanted to not give up on us, either. It's a shame I didn't have experience with this type of a relationship before. If I knew then what I know now, I could have saved myself the heartache of what followed in the weeks that came after.

I began to see less and less of him; our usual Date Nights on Saturday evenings were non-existent. Halfway through April, Mom brought it to my attention that we had not seen each other for three weeks. We were in touch; he would type to me when he wasn't off with a friend or with his relatives, but video chats simply weren't happening anymore. I mentioned this to him typing, "We haven't seen each other for a long time. I want to *see* you—*I miss you.*" Saturday, April 8, my calendar was clear and so was his: it was the perfect time. I was excited again, as I had been in the beginning. I even put on a dress that day, attempting to look nice for him.

My efforts were for naught. "A mate of mine just came over," he typed, "I'm sorry love, but I'm going to go out for a bit—weather here is too good to pass up." That hurt; disappointed, I simply told him to go enjoy the day and have fun, but inside my heart ached echoing, *"I want to see you—I miss you."* Thursday, April 13 was the last time I ever heard from him. He was going out, the start of the Easter celebration weekend for him, which meant getting a jumpstart on drinking, and said I would not hear from him at all with Monday being a "mystery." I know now that I fell into a miniature depression after seeing that: it felt like he was slipping further and further away from me, that he didn't want to be around anymore.

Naivety is, unfortunately, my greatest weakness—a side effect of my autism. I did not understand that by even suggesting the resolve of a break up, Kirk was telling me he was done, that, as far as he was concerned, we were over. (So much for being able to come to him with anything.) It was going on three in the morning now; I tossed and turned in my bed, unable to keep my eyes closed long enough to achieve sleep. My heart was weighed down with an indescribable heaviness, my eyes cloudy with tears. In a last desperate effort regarding my crumbling link to Kirk, I consulted Marinna: a very close friend, my best friend in fact, relaying everything that transpired between us. Her response gave me strength for what happened next.

I ended it on April 15, 2017.

It's been almost five months now, and it still feels so terribly strange, like it never happened at all. But my heart knows it did. Sometimes, late at night, for absolutely no reason at all, I find myself remembering him, imagining a life that could have been were it not for those fucking bottles, and a few tears let loose. I attempted to erase him—pictures, GIF files, and songs on YouTube he had sent, along with one I actually made—all of them were painful reminders that had to go before I lost my resolve. The worst to take down was the fake rose and huge card he had sent me on Valentine's Day; I had to stuff them into a drawer in our guest room, and I still have yet to throw them away.

Somehow, I can't seem to bring myself to do it—always going back and forth on following through with putting them in the trash, mostly because I forget I have them.

I also still have a white dress that I had bought: we planned to be Eric and Shelly from *The Crow* on Halloween when I was supposed to see him in Ireland. I suspect he might have had the intention to ask me to marry him then. He had been hinting the whole time that when I came over, there was something special he wanted very much to give me. I'll never know for sure, but something tells me I'm right. Again, I can't quite bring myself to get rid of it, either. I had told myself it was because I do love the dress, as it made me feel beautiful. I believe that's true; maybe, subconsciously, I can't let it go for other reasons. I don't know.

This experience was a terrible one that comes back on occasion to emotionally hurt me, but it did leave me with one very important underlying message: I am *not* trivial, and I *will* be loved when the time and, most importantly, *the person* is right.

Baring It All

Andrew Gurza

Ever since I was little, I've had someone seeing me naked as part of their job. In these instances, my body isn't beautiful—it's broken. They come into my home every morning and night, put on sterile gloves that smell like latex and plastic, with machine-like precision and purpose, and begin handling my body. They pull open my scissored legs to wash and dry me. They quickly and fervently move their hurried hands across every part of me, ensuring every single patch of skin and every single bit is properly tucked and trimmed, so that once I am up in my wheelchair, ready to start the day, or to spend an evening on the town, I look presentable. Their hands feel cold and clinical. During these moments, my body isn't really mine anymore. My naked body becomes little more than a thing to be taken care of; each part of me a checklist of steps that must be completed before we can move onto the next.

In some small way, I try to desensitize myself to this experience, trying not to feel as though I am nothing more than something that needs to be cleaned and clinically tended to. Living with cerebral palsy, and being a wheelchair user since the age of four, this routine has become second nature to me, and has made me look at nudity and nakedness as a necessary requirement in order to complete a care task; nothing more or less than that.

I understand these two systems quite well . . . now. I know that my queer, crippled body inhabits these two spaces simultaneously, and I have learned to navigate them well, and to compartmentalize my feelings in each space as required. It has taken me quite a long while to get to this place of understanding and acceptance of my body, but there was a time, not so long ago, when these two spaces came together in a rush of excitement, fear, anger, and pain that I won't soon forget. This moment in time undeniably shaped my relationship with my queerness and my disability. It transformed how I see myself as a man, and how other men see me. This moment was pivotal in my understanding of my body and what it means to me.

I was nineteen years old, and I had just moved away from home to go to university in a different city, six hours away. My family and I were excited, because this meant a newfound independence that I had been longing for most of my teenage years. I have always been very close with my family—our relationship and bond always strong, in part, thanks to my disability—but we were both in need of this change. It meant I would be on my own, with the assistance of attendant care workers, a mixture of young men and women trained in personal support work, made available by the university. It meant I would finally have a taste of freedom, and my family would be able to see me in a different light—as an independent, young man. That was an absolutely exhilarating feeling. I was also excited about something else. This was my chance to finally access my sexuality with other men, something I had been talking about and wanting desperately ever since I was fifteen years old. This was my chance to finally get naked with other men, and I was certainly going to capitalize on that experience.

I was in my dorm room at Carleton University, in Ottawa, Canada, for weeks every night. I was studying law as my major, with the hopes of going into law and disability. I enjoyed the academic part of school, but I often struggled when it came to the social aspects. Making friends wasn't easy for me. In fact, it still isn't. I was, as cliché as it sounds, a shy, awkward, queer, crippled kid. I had a few close friends I hung out with, but I never really connected with the campus LGBTQ+ crowd.

When classes let out, I would come back to my room and begin scouring the Internet, hoping to make this fantasy of mine a reality. I created profile after profile, trying to entice the right gentleman caller back to my quarters. Each and every time I would let them know I was a disabled man looking to get naked, have sex and see what happened, I was let down. They would tell me they wanted to, but they couldn't because of my disability: that it scared them too much, or they were worried they might hurt me.

These were excuses I had heard of people saying to disabled people before, but I never actually thought people really said that stuff! I was becoming considerably discouraged.

Over the next month or so, I would look at myself in the mirror before bed. I have always had a cheeky, nervous smile that creeps out from behind big, intense, hazel eyes. Some people have said I bear a bit of a resemblance to Tom Cruise in the eighties. As I look at my body twisting and curving around the confines of my wheelchair, I think to myself, in that moment, *Will any man ever want to see me naked? Will any man ever find me attractive?*

I wanted so badly to be touched in a way that was different than I had ever been before. In my head, I had fantastical daydreams of being swept up out of my wheelchair feverishly, and undressed by a beautiful man who wanted me just as much as I wanted him. I would picture queer porn stars like

Colby Keller, or actors like Heath Ledger or Mark Wahlberg. I imagined they would look at me, with all my noticeable flaws and imperfections, and despite all of them, they would fall in lust with my body and find the beauty in it no one else could. These little slices of heaven kept me going, determined to be naked with another man for the very first time.

One day, I was continuing my quest for unclothed companionship, and I wasn't having much luck in the matter. I was annoyed my polite demeanor online was getting me no closer to the clothing removal party I was wanting. I was typing things like, *Hey! You're cute. Do you wanna hang out?* I knew this wasn't the most direct line to nakedness, but I was trying to ease them into the idea of hanging out, *before* I disclosed my disability. Nothing was working.

My roommate, a young, straight man with a physical disability, and a wheelchair user himself, came home and poked his head in to see what I was doing. When he realized I was on a gay site looking for sex, he smirked and said, "You're doing that all wrong. You have to be much more concise and clear." He pushed me out of the way, and angled his way to the keyboard, "Here, try this." He began typing: *Disabled guy looking to get naked. Anybody wanna come over?* I remember feeling both exposed and angry that he had so unabashedly and openly disclosed my disability to the world. "There. That's how it's done. Now you'll get somewhere," he said, and left the room with a big, shit-eating grin on his face.

As he left the room, and I stared at the words blinking back at me on the screen, I was terrified. *Oh, my god. What if this works?* I thought. I had wanted it so much, the fantasy of being naked with another man, that I had failed to give any consideration to what might happen if it *actually happened*!

My roommate was right, though. It didn't take too long at all for me to start receiving responses to my brazen, bold call out for body contact. Every few minutes, my screen would *ding!* with an unmistakable noise that signified to me I might be closer to my goal of getting naked than I had anticipated. I was excited all of these men wanted to get naked with me, that I had disclosed my disability, and they still all wanted to spend time with me. This unmistakable mixture of emotions overwhelmed me, but I pushed them down as far as they could go into my throat, and I began leafing through my offers.

If I was going to get naked with a man, he had to be the "perfect" specimen (over the years, I have abandoned these unrealistic ideals of perfection, but I wasn't there just yet). I understood how important this moment really was for me. I couldn't share this moment with just *anyone* (I am totally aware of the irony of this statement, as I was looking to get naked with a man who I would ultimately meet off the computer). I wanted my fantasy man to jump out at me on the screen, the one who would ravage me from my wheelchair. Was one of these blinking messages approving my request for newfound nakedness from him?

As I scrolled through each of them, none really caught my attention. They were all considerably older than I was, and were proposing the filthiest of things we could do to one another. I was both flattered and kind of turned off by the whole idea. I just wanted a man to look at my naked, crippled body and enjoy what he saw. What I didn't want was to spend the afternoon with someone leering over me. I was just about to give up, shut off the laptop and go for a walk around campus to clear my head. "This was useless, and just was never meant to happen," I said to myself, as I packed up my things to leave for the afternoon, dismayed that, by now, I should be doing something else entirely. Just as I was about to open the automatic door to outside, I again heard that unmistakable *ding!* from my computer, it not being fully shut like I thought.

I whipped my wheelchair back around toward the noise, pulled back the screen and quickly scanned my mouse, and my eyes, on the box flashing in front of me. There was one lone message sitting in the chat window that said, *Hey. You were looking for someone to come over? I'd be interested. Definitely.* I froze. "What do I do now?" I questioned myself, quietly. I clicked on his picture, and to my surprise, my fantasy man was an actual person. He was beautiful, big, and muscular. He had brown, wavy hair, a flashy smile, and his private photo collection left little to my imagination. He seemed to be everything I wanted at the time. I sat staring at the keys trying to carefully craft a response that would seem cool, unencumbered, totally and utterly relaxed. *Hey there*, I typed, *Sure. I could hang out.* That was the kind of thing I am sure I wrote, although I can't verify that with any certainty, because all I can honestly remember is freaking out.

We exchanged a number of chat windows wherein I clearly laid out my disability, what I was looking for, and where I was located. He didn't seem at all fazed or taken aback by my wheelchair; in fact, he seemed kind of excited. He said he could be at my place in an hour so. I readily agreed, and began planning for this momentous occasion.

I started flailing, almost flying around my dorm room. I was banging open closet doors, calling the attendant, and telling them I needed to put on new clothes *NOW*. I made them rummage through my small dorm closet, which wasn't very big, in search of the perfect outfit. Together, in between fits of nerves and near hyperventilating, I picked an outfit that would be a) relaxed and casual, and b) easy enough for him to remove from my body. This was not a drill, and everything had to go smoothly. It had to be just right. *I* had to be just right. If I was going to be naked with a guy for the first time, nothing could go wrong, and I was going to make damn sure my disability didn't get in the way.

I remember going over to my mirror once again, and looking myself over from head to toe. I saw the wheelchair, like I always did, but this time I had this sense of relief and a new kind of confidence I hadn't experienced before. I was beaming with an unmistakable sense of pride. While I was really scared, I also believed I was totally ready for whatever went down. It was one of the moments you see in the movies, where the underdog has to psych himself up for the big game (that's pretty much the extent of my sports metaphors), except I was about to show a stranger I was a big gimp, in more ways than one (penis pun definitely intended).

During that hour—which seemed both unendingly long and severely short all at once—I also experienced several pangs of self-doubt. I could taste the fear in the lump in the back of my throat, as the moment inched closer. My hands were all clammy and felt like pins and needles. I didn't really know if I could do this at all. Could I really get naked in front of this guy, whose name I just learned? I couldn't shake the reality that, beneath all my bravado and self-imposed grandstanding, I was uncertain and uncomfortable with the idea of someone seeing me exposed like that. Up until this time in my life, I had been protected from all the mean-spirited remarks people make about the disabled, and now, here I was, going to show myself, my whole disabled self, to a stranger. There would be nothing and no one to protect me this time.

I waxed and waned, almost cancelling the whole thing three or four times before he arrived. Something inside me kept pushing me forward toward this moment. The next thing I knew, my old Nokia cellphone buzzed.

The buzzing snapped me back to reality, as I had been envisioning a million different possible scenarios coming true from this encounter: falling in love, having great sex, maybe even a relationship would start. *I'm here.* His text was succinct and to the point. I quickly wrote back, my spastic fingers working overtime, trying to reply. I wrote back something, letting him know I would be right there, my mind and body in a race for the door. As I grabbed my keys, and headed out, I caught a glimpse of myself in the mirror: baseball cap, a three-quarter-length shirt, track pants, and a killer smile. I looked at myself, gave a wry, nervous giggle, and headed down to the elevator bay. I pressed the button to go down, and waited for what felt like an eternity. When the doors finally opened, and I was safely sealed in solitary, I began talking to myself. I was reminding myself that no matter what happened, I would be okay. I heard the sound of the elevator as it made its way down. I watched each number, my chest tightening as I got closer to the ground floor. As it finished its descent, and I backed out of it, I scanned the lobby in search of the first man who would ever see my naked, disabled body.

When I finally spotted him, I couldn't contain the grin on my face, out of sheer excitement. He looked absolutely incredible. He was wearing jeans and a plaid shirt, accentuating his arms. I was so nervous approaching him. I could only hear my wheelchair whirring behind me as I inched closer. All my confidence was coming undone. I was barely able to say his name, as I introduced myself. We gave each other this strange half-hug (the one that says, "We just met, and now we're gonna fuck"), and he followed me to where the elevators were. As we stood inside the box together beside each other, the silence was deafening. It was filled with this pregnant anticipation I can only describe as electric. Neither of us said a word. As I quickly glanced in his direction, I stared at his frame. In fact, I couldn't take my eyes off him. I was excited to see what he would look like without clothes. I was ready to find out, and I hoped the same was true for him.

We made our way off the elevators, him quietly trailing me. The fact he wasn't speaking at all made me even more nervous, but I didn't want to ruin what was hopefully to come. "And, here we are," I said, as I opened the door to the dorm, wheeling right into my bedroom and ushering him in with me. He came toward me and grabbed my face in a gentle embrace, signifying we were to begin. I responded by ravenously clawing at him, wanting to unwrap the package underneath. He smiled, and told me to slow down. He reminded me it was okay to take our time at this.

He was about take off my shirt, when he stopped. I was sure he was about to realize this was all too much for him to take; the disabled guy in the big, bulky chair. He was going to leave; I just knew it. *Awwwww, fuck*, I thought to myself. To my surprise, he simply said, "I've never undressed anyone before like this. What do I do?" I breathed a giant, welcome sigh of relief. I was happy he wasn't going anywhere, but I was also acutely aware of the fact my disability was going to be a part of this experience whether I wanted it to or not. The two of us fumbled around one another for a minute, and eventually I was able to tell him what needed to be done. He pushed my stiff body forward, pulling me forward revealing the scar going from the top of my shoulder blades to my bum, as my shirt came off.

There I sat in my wheelchair, half naked. I had been half-dressed like this many times before now, but this was the very first time it wasn't because I needed personal care at all. I was half-naked because this guy, standing in front of me, wanted me to be. He took his shirt off, too, and it was one of the most exciting moments. As I watched him, trying to look as unaffected as possible, the frame I noticed underneath his shirt came into focus. I was not disappointed.

He moved toward me more purposefully now. We quickly kissed again, as he asked me how I needed help into bed. I stammered and stuttered trying to give him easy directions to follow, but I was having a considerably difficult time of it, because usually I am relaying this information to someone who is gloved, prepped and ready to provide me with care; they are not standing in front of me looking like a Norse God.

I told him what he needed to do, and he put me in bed. He slowly came in next to me. He moved his hands around my bare chest. I remember he smelled like this intoxicating mixture of deodorant and sweat, covering me with the warmth of his body. This touch felt different. This felt new. His touch was firm, but soft. For the very first time, I was learning what it meant to be touched out of want.

Next, he wanted to take off my pants. This is always an interesting exercise, as it involves a considerable amount of rolling and twisting. I guided him as to what to do, and he slowly took off my track pants, the only type of pants I wore, because it's much more comfortable for someone who sits eighteen hours a day. He rolled me back and forth as I directed him, and it became this weird dance between the two of us, a mixture of instruction and intimacy. I remember being slightly angered by the fact that the extraction of my pants didn't fall in line with the fantasy I had in my head. Again, I was confronted with my crippledness.

Right then, I understood I was completely naked. I felt a small draft of air travel down the nape of my neck and rest on my backside. He rolled me back over with a gentle but firm aggression. I remember looking at him expectantly. *Well, here I am*, my inner voice chimed in my head. I was lying flat on my back, completely nude. My arms full of spasticity rest upon either side of my chest. My chest, speckled with a smattering of hair, heaved up and down, taking in the intensity of this moment. As I looked down further, my penis was standing at attention. Sometimes unwanted erections would happen during my attendant care, and I would flush with redness, and become completely embarrassed. I had been taught that receiving personal care was a professional act, and so I took great pains to remember that at all times. Right here, in this moment, though, it was different. I was allowed to be excited here. I was allowed to enjoy this.

He looked at me, and positioned himself next to me. I was recording this moment in my head. Trying to remember every detail, because it was a significantly sexy milestone for me. As he took off his pants, and we lay there together, I remember thinking how important this was. I wanted it to mean so much. It was the first moment that my queer, crip identities were on the same collision course. It was the first time I felt sexy. It was the very first time somebody looked at me while I was naked, and didn't try to diagnose or deal with my disability. I could just be myself here, and let it all loose.

My nakedness was liberating in this moment, but as I had expected, I was also concerned that all that my nakedness entailed—curves, scars, divots, and the unmistakable markings that make up disability—would be too real for my lover to handle. He didn't flinch at all. We had sex while his hands felt my body, and I grabbed at his, feeling free. When we were done, I had such a surge of energy and empowerment. The little, queer, crippled kid finally got some. He lay on top of me, and I looked up at him beaming with a boyhood giddiness that wouldn't subside.

With this fresh surge of confidence, I decided to tell him I'd like to see him again. "Would you want to hang out again sometime? I'd like to see you again." I'll never forget the look on his face. He got up on his haunches, and got jumpy, the way I had seen guys in the movies do when they are about to leave the girl high and dry. "Oh. Well, you see your wheelchair there?" He pointed to my chair, as he pulled his pants up off the floor and quickly put them on. I nodded yes. "Well, I just came by because I felt bad for you. You were just a pity fuck."

As I heard the words leave his lips, I just swallowed hard, barely able to squeak out the meek "Okay" that I did. I couldn't believe what had just happened. There I was, my first time physically naked with a man, my first time accessing who I am, my first attempt at real sex, my first attempt at manhood, and *this* is what he says?!

He gave me one last look, and asked me if there was anything more I needed from him. I asked him to give me the phone on my dresser. He mumbled some sort of goodbye, but at this point I wasn't even looking at him, because I was trying not to cry. I heard the door click closed. I grabbed the covers and pulled them up, covering my naked body as much as I could. I was so, so angry. I was angry with myself for being so gullible and naive, angry with him for saying what he said, and I was angry that I had to have a disability at all. The magical world I had imagined coming to life, full of sex and love, had instead come crashing down right on my head. It wasn't supposed to happen this way. He was supposed to go riding on the back of my wheelchair into the sunset, professing his love in sonnets and poems and all that romanticized bullshit, right? Instead, I was lying there in a puddle of my own tears and shame, crumpled up with my crippled identity all alone. What had gone wrong?

I was the angriest because I had let him in. I showed him how to be with me. I showed him how my disability was a part of me; even as I was learning that lesson myself. When he saw who I was and what that *really* meant, he got scared and left. Didn't he know I was just as scared? Didn't he know I just wanted a little more time so he wouldn't be scared of me after all?

It was a moment in my development as a queer, disabled man that I will hold close to me for the rest of my life. For some time after that, the idea of getting naked for pleasure again repulsed me. I took great comfort in disrobing only when necessary, and only when it was accompanied with a reason that was directly related to my care needs. I was terrified anything other than that would lead to these painful consequences, and I wasn't sure I could handle that again.

As I look back on the experience, some thirteen years later, I am so glad I was able to bare all to someone like that. I learned a valuable lesson that day, one I keep with me every time I get naked from now on. I learned when you are disabled, and you *choose* to get naked in front of someone, you are doing so much more than just removing your clothes. You are showing them who you are. You are removing your costume, which helps you to play the part of a "normal" person in the world; taking off the things that hide your true identity, owning your disability for all that it is. You are sharing with them something so special and rare, they might not know how to handle it. By getting naked with them, you are being real with them, hoping they will tap into that vulnerability with you. It is only the lucky few who will. Ultimately, though, being naked for the first time with a man was a stepping stone for me as a queer, disabled man. It showed me when I get naked with someone, I am not just showing you my body. If you look a little bit closer, you may just see my soul.

Sleeveless At Least

Teresa M. Elguézabal

Before my radio alarm turned on NPR's *Morning Edition*, I woke up jittery. It was early, and still dark outside, but I didn't want to risk falling back asleep. So I rolled out of bed and took my time dressing in my lady lawyer clothes—a boxy suit and sensible pumps. I listened to the news: something about George W. Bush's recent re-election and the traffic report. Then I set off walking from my Baltimore home to the neighborhood bus stop. My briefcase, laden with documents for my hearing, hung from my shoulder.

Along my familiar route, the flip of my hair measured time against my neck. On sunny days, I had exaggerated my stride and watched my hair in the shadows. That morning, though, it was too early for the sun's shadows. Passing cars had their headlights on.

Just how I got hit, I can't say, because a concussion carved out a slice of what I should remember. Over and over, I have tried to imagine the moments as the car gained on me. The halo cast by the headlights must have grown with each rotation of the wheels. Did I run or freeze in place? Or did I panic like a squirrel, scampering back and forth in the road? Four years after the accident, the driver, himself, would tell me that the hit made me spin. And then I dropped. Thinking back to that still-dark winter morning, Thursday, December 9, 2004, *I wish I had overslept.*

Whenever people asked about the accident, I began the answer with: "The night before, I went dancing." On Wednesday nights, I routinely met up with *tangueros* at Gardel's, a restaurant-bar and dance club located off President Street in east Baltimore. Tango was my new passion and escape from the stress of my working life. It was fun. So, I put on a burgundy, sleeveless dress and lipstick, fussed with my hair, and drove to Gardel's. I couldn't stay late, because the next morning I was scheduled to join a colleague, also a Maryland assistant attorney general, in court for a hearing.

At Gardel's, a man from across the room caught my eye, and, with a barely discernible nod, he indicated, *Want to?* Clad in my burgundy sheath, with a slit up my thigh, I joined him on the dance floor. Toward the end of the song, he strengthened his embrace signaling to hold on. As he stepped back, I leaned into his chest. My leg swerved out through the slit in my dress. Fast—three seconds, tops—and upright, my show-off leg returned to its place.

Nearby diners clapped.

Surprised, I took a little bow and went home to sleep.

Why did I roll out of bed early in the morning? I should have danced until bar-closing time and, with luck, I would have overslept. Not showing up for court because I'd been out late *milongueando* would have made juicy gossip. I could have lived with the label *irresponsible*, even if I'd gotten fired. Instead, I missed court because I had to be loaded, head first, into an ambulance.

***

Life-sustaining equipment and medical tubes cluttered the space in and around my bed. Sitting up, I squeezed an exercise ball, feeling my flaccid bicep contract and relax --*twenty-one, twenty-two, twenty-three* ... By then, I had survived a stint in a Baltimore shock trauma unit and had been moved out of ICU. Yet, I was still nourished with a milkshake concoction plunged into a gastric tube. A catheter emptied my bladder. A ventilator breathed for me through a hole in my neck, making a roar that my three-year-old grandson said was "like Darth Vader." An orthopedic brace hugged my left ankle.

Family visited me often. My grandson Ari was tall enough that I could hug him as he stood next to my bed. But my daughter, Andrea, had to lift one-year-old Gabe, his legs flailing inches over my chest, while I kissed him. My brothers and sisters and my dad had flown in from Oregon, and were in and out of my room.

As I exercised my arms, I was alone, until a young doctor making rounds walked in. Glancing at the exercise ball in my hand, she flashed me a smile. "Keep that up," she said. "Upper-body strength will help you later to operate your wheelchair."

My jaw tightened. Although it wasn't like me to throw the F-word around, "FUCK!" is what I said. Despite the breathing tube in my neck, I let out a gravelly, "I have to dance." I struggled to say I was toning my arms to wear sleeveless blouses at *milongas*. The doctor shrugged and busied herself with my drips, the liquids flowing out of clear sacks on a metal pole and entering my veins. "You have to be prepared ..." she said, and "Don't fool yourself." After she left, I whimpered like a lost child.

My dad walked in, stopped about ten feet away, and sighed. Even at age seventy-eight, he struck an imposing figure. He wore his usual garb: a western-style, long-sleeved shirt, with snaps instead of buttons, and his white cowboy hat. I waved him over and told him what the doctor said about a wheelchair. His face flushed with anger: "No believe it," he said, in his English mixed with Spanish syntax. *No believe it.*

"Papi, *abrázeme*," I said—hug me. I addressed him by the diminutive Papi *(paw-pea)*, like I did when I was little. I yearned for his comfort, to feel his flesh and bones against mine. He tried, leaning over me and my tubes, but his upper lip quivered and he rushed out before I could see my *macho* dad cry. "*Los hombres no lloran*" was one of his refrains. *Ay, Papi*, I wanted to tell him—real men cry, too. Had my mother been alive, she would have held me tight, sobbing without shame until she hiccupped and had to drink water.

Reaching for the exercise ball, I squeezed it with all I had.

***

I was infatuated with Argentine tango—it's rituals, language, and music. Dress code for women is sexy—scooped necklines, open backs, and cropped tank tops. As a grandma, I kept to sleeveless, so that, at least, my shoulders would go bare. A *milonga* is a tango party and *cabeceo* the subtle nod by which one invites another to dance. We dance a *tanda* (four consecutive songs with the same person) and *cortina* (a snippet of non-tango music) signals the end of the *tanda*, when dancers change partners. Names of the dance steps are whimsical: *ochos cortados* (interrupted figure eights), *cunita* (cradle), *gancho* (hook), and *la mordidita* (the nibble). And tango music by orchestras like Pugliese, Di Sarli, and musician Yo-Yo Ma added worldliness to my play list. I was head over heels for tango.

Dancing tango is like jazz—improvised. The order of steps, or whether a certain step is danced at all, depends on the music, the floor space, and the mood of the dancers. In tango, the stillness of *la pausa*, makes for soulful dancing. Directional shifts in the dance are communicated through the body, ideally the heart. I also relied on the sensation of my partner's arm on my back and his hand in mine. Either way, we seldom talk while dancing, because we are listening to the body whispers of our partners and replying with our own murmurs.

***

Wearing blue scrubs, she entered my room and altered the course of my recovery. She pressed my bed's control to sit me upright. "I'm Brenda from PT," she said and shook my hand. "Patients call me the mean one," she added. "I expect you to work." I liked this physical therapist—perky, yet no-nonsense.

On our first day, Brenda helped me sit on my bed's edge with my legs dangling. I felt woozy and leaned to the side. By force of strength, she held me up. She was tough for a petite woman. Given her hands-on approach, no wonder her brown curly hair looked uncombed. "You have to sit before you can stand," she said. "You've been in bed too long."

Five months, to be exact. Although I had already been weaned off the ventilator and was eating real food, chronic vomiting and infections kept me in bed. Another reason I hadn't walked was "contractions." The muscles and ligaments around my knees had tightened, so my knees didn't bend much. Other physical therapists had tried manual stretches, pressing my thigh down and my calf backwards like they were closing rusty garden clippers. If that helped, I couldn't tell.

Brenda planned to get me out of bed and walking.

I liked that. *If I could walk, I could dance.*

The second week Brenda worked with me, an assistant joined her. Marvin brought along a wheelchair. First, she helped me put on a second gown to open in front over the one I already wore that opened in back. "This way, you won't moon anyone," she said --funny and considerate of my dignity, too. Then she and Marvin lowered me into the wheelchair and rolled me to a therapy gym where patients exercised on treadmills and stationary bicycles. They wore sweatpants, t-shirts, and sneakers. I wore two flimsy gowns and socks with grip-strips on the soles. *What was I doing here?*

Brenda positioned my wheelchair between parallel bars about twenty feet long. She locked my wheels, and then said, "Grab one bar with each hand, firmly." I did, and she checked my grip. "Now pull yourself up."

Because my legs extended out in front, I pulled with my scrawny arms, scooting my feet back inch by inch until they were under me and I was standing.

"Stand for one minute," Brenda said. "Hang on."

My stomach grumbled, but we kept counting the seconds. *Forty-nine Mississippi, fifty Mississippi.* Sweat beaded around my mouth. Marvin looked at my face and, from a nearby shelf, grabbed a pink plastic bucket. *Fifty-nine . . . sixty,* and I sat. Thick saliva collected in my mouth. I tasted bile. Just in time, Marvin placed the bucket in my lap and gave me a towel. Someone handed me a water bottle, and Brenda rubbed my shoulders.

Then she said, "Stand up again. Come on, take a few steps."

I did my awkward pull-up on the parallel bars, and, with flat-footed steps, walked. Brenda stayed next to me counting my steps and coaching me. "Heel-toe, heel-toe. Use your whole foot." And, "Bend your knees. You can bend more. Bend." Marvin followed behind with the wheelchair. Nearing the end of the parallel bars, Brenda asked if I wanted to sit.

"No." Wobbling, I turned around, ready to make a run for it—in a manner of speaking.

Marvin pulled the wheelchair back and rushed around the parallel bars to get behind me going the other direction. Back where I started, I sat, exhausted yet invigorated.

The Fats Domino tune and lyrics—*I'm walkin'/yes, indeed*—played in my head. I imagined my leg sweeping a short *barrida* and flowing through a low-to-the-floor *boleo*. My subconscious, it seemed, was resigned—no long strides or high leg lifts for me. Now that I was taking baby steps, I could envision going home. And then—tango.

There are therapeutic benefits to dancing. Tango, in particular, is thought to be helpful for patients with neurological diseases like Parkinson's. With its smooth walking steps and supportive embrace, tango improves fluidity of movement. It also enhances brain function, because improvised movements demand focus. And tango's custom of changing partners keeps our minds flexible.

An article I came upon was aptly titled, "Feeling Blue? Try Tango." I'll vouch for that. Even as I used to get ready for dancing, my face glowed. Makeup had nothing to do with it, because my only cosmetic was lipstick. Tango boosts our spirits with physical closeness between lovers, friends, and strangers alike. We hold each other to music, our heads touching at the temples. And dancing four consecutive songs with the same person deepens the connection, now and then simulating the euphoria of falling in love. *Oh yes, indeed.*

***

"Discharged" wasn't the right word. After eight months of hospital confinement, "released" on probation was more like it. As Andrea drove, she cheered, "You're out, Mom! You're going home!" Like a newcomer to town, I took in the advertisements along the road. One billboard caught my attention for its stark white background with black letters: BELIEVE.

Closer to home, I almost told Andrea to drive around the intersection where I was almost killed. But the site was my neighbor, and I'd have to face it sooner or later. I gripped the armrest. The flood of headlights and sounds of metal crashing might burst through in a PTSD episode. No such thing happened. Even at the crosswalk, I felt no urge to cry. No heart palpitations. No sweaty palms. No buried flashback.

On the public bench at the bus stop, I read the engraved lettering, "Baltimore, Greatest City in America." That slogan and the BELIEVE signs on billboards and bumper stickers were affirmations for a city sorely in need of healing, like me.

Andrea parked in the alley so I could walk on a flat sidewalk to my front door. Even the sidewalk, with tufts of grass growing out of cracks, was difficult with my walker. As I hobbled along with Andrea behind me, I said, "I wonder if the ramp is up." The day before, the contractor had called about the precise time of my discharge so he could install it in time. Andrea ran ahead to check, and, from around a bend, she yelled, "Wow! It's a contraption."

Upon seeing it, I froze: *Welcome home, gimp.* Shaped like a number 7, the ramp was configured from black, mesh metal pieces, rectangles and squares on stilts. Andrea walked up first and unlocked the door. Contraption or not, it was my only way in. So I swallowed hard, rolled up with my walker, and I was home.

Home was not how I'd left it. Instead of centered in the room under the chandelier, my dining room table was pushed against a wall. The computer sat on a corner of the table. Area rugs were rolled and shoved out of the way so I couldn't trip. Only two dining chairs remained. The rest had been stored in the basement to make room for a hospital bed and a wheelchair. That chair gave me the creeps. I didn't need it, but my discharge plan called for it, just in case. In the first-floor bathroom, an elevated commode with arms had been installed over the toilet. *Ay-ay-ay!* I would dance again in *the greatest city in America.* In that I had to BELIEVE.

Soon after my return home, a tango buddy started warming me up to the idea—"You're going to the *milonga*, right?" She had to be kidding. Having lost forty pounds, I looked boney and wan. My shoulders scrunched up from leaning over the walker. And with little knee flexibility, I felt like a stick woman. "I'll get you there," Laurie said. "It will do you good to watch." I wasn't sure.

Yet my tango memories occupied my imagination and dreams. Dancing in close embrace, our heartbeats became whispers: *We have each other and nothing else.* With languid strides, we walked in the cross system—stepping between thighs. Then our feet arrived at *cruzada*, ankles crossed where the current can change. Life is brutal, but my passion for tango, no one can take it away.

"Okay," I told Laurie, "I'll go."

My first *milonga* after I became disabled was on a college campus, at a social hall known as The Barn. Getting me there required coordination. To begin with, what could I wear? My clothes were baggy. A friend volunteered to shop for me. I asked for a black, fitted tank top, shimmery, if she saw one, because dress code is sexy—sleeveless (at least). A non-dancing friend would drive Laurie and me to The Barn, and take me home early. Someone else found a walking route to The Barn that avoided stairs, but there was a catch. Laurie called ahead to alert campus security that our vehicle would be driving on sidewalks because one passenger was disabled.

Upon arrival, Laurie used my cushion to elevate a chair for me, and friends came by to greet me. Someone said,

"You're brave, not everyone can survive what you've been through." But I didn't deserve a medal of courage. I had made no difficult choices. I merely endured.

A man I knew nodded at me with an inviting eyebrow shrug. I recoiled, but Laurie nudged me—"Try it, see how it goes." I struggled to stand and people helped me.

On the dance floor, I managed tentative steps, backwards and forward—not even to the music. From the sidelines, people watched my curious sideshow. Someone tapped my partner's back to cut in. Then someone else did. On and off, throughout my time at the *milonga*, one *tanguero* or another stepped forward to dance with me, as if it was my birthday.

And it was—a different sort of birth day.

***

At home, I settled into my outpatient life. To doctor and physical therapy appointments, I traveled in a medical transport van. Paid personal care attendants helped me during the day. Relatives visited for a week or two at a time. Neighbors brought me rotisserie chickens. Two little boys liked to run up and down my ramp, making the Tarzan-like yelp with the momentum of the down slope. I had what the law calls an "attractive nuisance." Fortunately, the little boys never got hurt.

One day, my thirty-something neighbor came over with wine. When I asked what she was celebrating, she said, with a mischievous grin, "You." I shook my head. "You make me feel great," she said, "and you're convenient, too." When she gets blue about life, she explained, she walks out of her house and looks at my ramp. "Just like that," she said, as she snapped her fingers, "and I'm not so bad off after all." *Jerk*, I wanted to say, *try counseling or tango for the blues and leave my crooked legs out of it.* But I couldn't alienate a friendly neighbor. Besides, she had merely expressed a plain truth: I evoked gratitude in others for the simple reason that their lives were not as shitty as mine.

***

Thinking about general anesthesia and the ventilator sprouted goose bumps on my arms. After six months of outpatient physical therapy, I consulted an orthopedic surgeon. My daughter Andrea, with two-year-old Gabe in her arms, accompanied me, as did a case manager from my insurance company. A nurse helped me onto the examination table.

When the surgeon walked in, he poked the stuffed bear in my grandson's hand. That playful gesture put me at ease. "What brings you here?" the surgeon asked, and I summarized—the car, the marathon hospitalization, and my unbending knees. I said my right knee had improved with physical therapy. "As for my stubborn left knee, I need your help."

I had many questions about post-surgery rehab. Could I live alone in my house? Or would I need live-in help? Although my daughter lived in town, she was married and had two little boys. "Assuming the operation goes well," I said, "what limitations will I have?"

"Well," he chortled, "you'll never be on *Dancing with the Stars.*"

I burst into tears. (So much for putting me at ease.)

He glanced at my daughter.

"Dancing is my mom's passion," Andrea said. "Mom used to dance three times a week."

He turned to me. "Oh . . . uh . . . I'm sorry."

I didn't expect to dance at the same level as before, but *I had to dance.* I would accept leaving *milongas* early and dancing once or twice a month. I didn't need fancy steps. I'd be grateful to dance *sleeveless (at least)*.

I told the surgeon about my hip pain. "My hips also make a grinding sound when I sit."

His eyes widened. Recently, when I had told my rehab doctor, she called my noisy hips music to her ears—said it meant the contracted tissues were loosening up.

"Lie on your side," the surgeon said. Then he placed his ear on my hip. "Bend your top knee." I did and he heard it. He listened to my other hip—same thing.

I was sent to Imaging. In a half hour, the surgeon called me back. On the opaque frame on the wall that lit from behind, he displayed the X-ray image of one hip. "There's no other way to say this, but bluntly," he said. "You also need two total hip replacements."

My breath grew shallow. I didn't cry.

"Right here," he said, pointing to the pencil-thin line on the image between the thighbone and pelvis. "There's usually space here that would be cartilage. You've lost your cartilage," he said. "So your bones scrape against each other." The film of my other hip showed the same problem.

Why did my cartilage wear off? A couple of reasons: long-term immobility, and, due to my restricted knees, I'd been overusing my hips.

Days after I received word of two additional operations, I met with my physical rehab doctor. She looked sheepish, and began the conversation with, "So, bilateral hip replacements, huh?"

"That's right," I practically shouted. "What you called *music to your ears* were my bones scraping each other."

The rehab doctor said nothing. My case manager stared at the floor.

My thoughts turned to Barbaro, the bay colt who had recently shattered his right hind leg during the 2006 Preakness. Watching on television, I had wept as the horse fell. Fans in the stands had chanted, *"Don't shoot that horse."* Photographs in the news of a standing Barbaro holding one leg looked eerily familiar. Standing in place, I shifted all my weight to my right leg.

"If I were a horse," I said to my rehab doctor, "I'd be shot."

The air in the room felt stale and tepid. The rehab doctor didn't utter one word. My case manager leaned toward me: "You're not a horse, and shooting is not a treatment option."

"It's more humane."

***

The proverbial couch sat too low for me. So the psychiatrist brought in a tall wooden chair for me to sit with my walker in front. He sat across from me with a notepad on his lap.

"Do you understand why you were referred to me?"

Nodding, I said, "Because I said shooting me would be humane. They shoot horses like me."

"Why would you say something like that?"

I took a deep breath. "I went to a surgeon about one operation and was blasted with the news that I needed three. I'm a high risk for infections. Every infection you can get in the hospital found me. Sepsis twice. I could end up on life support again and not make it. So, why bother?—that thought entered, but it's left my mind."

He asked if I owned a gun or knew someone who did.

"No. I don't plan to *off* myself," I said. "I remember my daughter's grief when her father died. I won't put her through that, not on purpose. Plus, I adore my grandsons." I paused for him to catch up with his note taking. Then I gushed about the boys, ages four and two by then. "They're stunning. Alert, both of them. I want to teach them to dance." The psychiatrist read from my referral report. "There's probably no tango in heaven," I added, and chuckled at my own joke. No guarantee of heaven either, but I kept that to myself.

Psychiatrist cleared his throat. "I see you're not married. Do you have a boyfriend?"

I slapped my forehead. "Who'd want me like this?" I'd become an extreme version of the protagonist in the soap opera, *La que no podía amar*, the woman who couldn't love.

"What about desire?" he asked. "Do you feel it?"

Humiliating question! In retrospect, the inquiry was pertinent. An appetite would have shown I had gumption to live a full life for a woman in my fifties.

"Yes," I said, to shut him up. Truth was, I'd had *nada de nada*—negative nothingness. Wait . . . did yearning for tango count? I almost changed my "Yes" to "I don't know." But, then he'd write in his clinical note that I was utterly devoid of sexy—that I was *not even sleeveless*.

Al-though, I did have a visitor in my plans.

On the scheduled spring afternoon, I spotted him through my window: his tall frame, his sleeves folded to his elbows. Theo carried a wine bottle as he walked up my handicap ramp. Our visit had been planned well before the shrink quizzed me about my non-existent love life. Theo had been a dance partner when I had frequented the *milongas* in Washington, D.C. We were friends. We had never dated. We stayed in touch primarily through email. Today's plan was for dinner out.

Inside the door, he said, "Hi-i-i," as he looked me over. He hugged me, and then raised the bottle. "Let's open this." I walked him through the dining room with my elevated twin bed. In the kitchen, he poured two glasses and carried them to the living room.

"Put them there," I said, pointing to the massage table in front of the couch.

He sat on the end of the couch nearest the wheelchair, which I used only for sitting. With the walker, I backed up to the chair, gripped its arms, and warned him: "You get to hear my hips." As I lowered myself, he furrowed his brow at the grinding noise.

"That's your hips?"

Later in the evening, when we returned from dinner, Theo sat on the couch with his laptop to show me pictures of his recent travels. Mesmerized by his company, I forgot my miserable condition and plopped myself next to him. Sharp hip pain made me wince. I should have sat in the wheelchair.

"Theo, this low seat is killing my hips."

He tried to help, but I put my palm up for him to stand back.

Scooting to the edge of my seat, I bent one knee, but my other leg extended in front. With my hands on the couch's edge, I lifted some, but fell back.

He offered his arms. "Where should I hold?" I suggested under each elbow. "It won't happen," he said. "The angles aren't right." And he reached under my armpits and, with astonishing ease, lifted me. A quick pivot and he stood me in front of the massage table, with which I wanted to cover my face. *(His hands in my pits, for crying out loud!)*

"Do you want me to leave?" he asked.

I shook my head, and he held me until I reached for the walker and hobbled to sit on my bed's edge. Theo walked to the kitchen. "I'd like wine. Want a glass?" I didn't. Then he placed a dining room chair across from me and sat, looking handsome with his salt and pepper hair and sipping wine. And there I was.

Laughter poured out of me.

"What?" he said. "What's so funny?" Theo didn't even smile—"What is it?"

I explained: "If someone asks you about tonight, you'll say, 'I had to pick up a poor woman from the couch.'—*She got that drunk?*—'No, she has no hips.' That's what you'll say."

"Oh no." He shook his head. "Not a word. Don't worry. No."

"I'm thirsty," I said. He offered to bring me water, but I needed to move a little. When I returned to my perch, I asked, "Want to hear about my pre-op class?" He didn't say no, so I went right ahead. "I held a hip prosthesis in my hands." I swiveled a fist in my other cupped hand to show how the ball and socket joint works. Theo had known my hips through tango, he'd known the tease of our intertwining thighs.

"You know what's sad?" I heard sorrow in my voice. "I used to like my hips."

"So did I," he said, and, cradling the bowl of his wine glass, he held my gaze. That gaze started it, and then a supple warmth filled my mouth. So my answer that, "Yes," I felt desire had been true. "I miss dancing," I said.

He leaned toward me: "That's why you're having surgery."

I described the parts of the hip implant: the shallow metal cup that would become the new socket and the shank with a ball on one end. "Once the damaged bones are removed," I said, "the shank gets inserted in the hollow of my femur. Good grief . . . What am I describing?" I struggled to keep a straight face.

Laughing, Theo raised his wine glass: "To your new hips."

***

Two hip replacements—check. Knee surgery still in the queue.

My niece Victoria drove me to the *milonga*. She had been taking a gap semester off from college and had become my live-in attendant while I recovered from hip replacements. I wanted to show her that tango is a wonderful thing. She brought along her camera.

At Gardel's, I hung my cane on the back of a chair, and sat with Victoria to watch. I was less frail than a year ago when a team of friends had to help me at The Barn. Also, I walked with more autonomy. Credit belonged to my hip implants, which eliminated my cringe-inducing pain. Best of all, my hips were quiet.

Still, I drew attention. Glancing at my cane, one friend said, "Teresa, you've got balls." My hand clenched. I didn't need testicles to have grit and mettle. *Let it go*, I told myself— it was a common expression. *Why was I so prickly?*

The DJ, someone I'd danced with before I was injured, came over to chat. During my eight-month-long hospitalization, Curt had burned tango CDs for me, labeled them "Tango Therapy Disc 1" and 2, 3, 4, 5—a veritable library of tango music to jump-start my healing. At Gardel's, Curt tapped my hand: "If I play something gentle," he said, "are you up to walking around the floor with me?" The hairs on my forearms lifted. *Walking*, he said, not *dance*—that prickliness again. It seemed the super-attention I required to walk was affecting other aspects of my life. Listening with high-resolution audio, I picked up the jarring chords of every-day speech and unintended slights as well.

"Yes, Curt," I said. "I'll dance."

I was bombarded by disconnected stimuli. The slippery floor. My tense arm around his shoulder. Melody. Silly lyrics. *Boleos* of other dancers blurred in and out of my peripheral vision. To walk again, I'd had to break down the process into small components—*heel-toe, heel-toe*. That choppiness followed me as I stepped through *molinete* (grapevine). A few *ochos cortados* (interrupted figure eights). I didn't flow. Short steps and pauses. "Not bad," Curt said. Then I noticed men at the bar staring—*A woman with a cane limps into a bar* . . . and felt like a joke.

Back at the table, a smiling Victoria offered me her camera. "Look," she said. "You dance better than you walk." *Dance*, she said, bless her heart. I looked at the video: my limp was all but gone. At first, that seemed counter-intuitive. Dancing is more difficult than walking, right? Yet it made sense. When dancing, I had my partner's support and the music propelled me along. What a wonderful thing! My intent had been to show my niece tango. Instead, tango showed me.

***

My knee operation turned complicated. In addition to a knee a replacement, I required ligament reconstruction. Lucky for me that Perseverance had become my middle name. So I toughed it out and muddled through. Toward the end of my rehab, news of the presidential race between John McCain and Barack Obama was sizzling across NPR's *Morning Edition*, the cable networks, and YouTube.

My personal news was hot, too. I retired my walker and cane. I gifted the wheelchair to the elderly father of the woman who cleaned my house. The handicap ramp at my front door was dismantled. To casual observers, my permanent disabilities didn't show.

Yet I was (and, to this day, continue to be) disabled. A physical rehab doctor who evaluated my permanent disabilities concluded I had thirty-five percent impairment of my right leg and seventy percent impairment of my left leg. In addition, five percent impairment due to pelvic injuries (fractures from the accident) and nine percent impairment due to "gait disturbance."

What did this mean? That my walking posture was stiff and a little tilted. Although I now had functional hips and knees, I still had reduced range of motion. "No extreme or sudden moves with your legs," my surgeon had warned. I couldn't run, hop, skip, or squat. So I couldn't chase after my grandsons in the park or attempt a jump shot in their driveway. I would not jump rope with my granddaughter Elana (born three years after my accident). No more tennis. Nor could I run from a mugger or kick him in the balls. I could go on about what I've lost, but that doesn't serve me.

With my remaining capacity and sensible precautions, many worthy endeavors are open to me. I took up yoga. I started swimming and piano lessons. For my baby granddaughter, I practiced walking with a ten-pound bag of flour in my arms, so I could carry her without losing my balance. When Andrea returned to work, I picked up the kids after school and helped with homework. With friends, I enjoyed dinners out, movies, and plays. All by myself, I could stand up from the couch.

To dance, I pushed my capacity right to its edge.

At my first few *milongas* after surgeries and rehab, I heard the surgeon's words: *You'll never be on Dancing with the Stars.* Shaking my head, I repeated my mantras: *I'll find other stars,* or, when feeling full of myself, *I am the star.*

Clad in a black sleeveless top, trumpet skirt, and green shoes with wide ankle straps, I danced. My partner for this *tanda* was masterful with pauses at the end of musical phrases, tapping his foot for a beat or two before moving on. Between songs in the *tanda*, I complimented his precision, his footwork, and he said, "I like your *presence.*" Had he been effusive with praise, I wouldn't have believed him.

Out of necessity, I danced with greater awareness or *presence*. In fact, with all my life functions, I have become more deliberate, compensating for lost range of motion with heightened mindfulness and focus. Before I became disabled, I had taken my good legs for granted, sometimes letting my mind wander to the summary judgment paper I had to file with the court. Now I stayed in the dance moment.

My feet pivoted through *ochos*. With tiny steps, we cradled *cunita*. My leg reached back, followed by a *boleo* close to the floor. Curving around the room, I reached my capacity's edge and lagged behind. "Oops." I was off-center, but realigned. "We made it work," he said. Smooth dancing—his feet hugged my foot in *sandwichito*, released it. We paused to dance in stillness, no rush. I should have danced like this all along. Then it happened—I entered that rare tango zone, a meditative trance when my legs feel weightless. And I danced on a sky lit by millions of stars.

About the Editor

Belo Miguel Cipriani is a columnist with the Bay Area Reporter. In 2017, his column on disability issues was recognized by the National Center on Disability and Journalism at the Walter Cronkite School of Journalism at Arizona State University.

He is the author of *Blind: A Memoir* (2011), which received an Honorable Mention for Best Nonfiction Book by the 2011 Rainbow Awards, and an Honorable Mention for Best Culture Book by the 2012 Eric Hoffer Awards.

He has received fellowships from Lambda Literary and Yaddo, and was the first blind writer to attend the Bread Loaf Writers' Conference. Cipriani has guest lectured at Yale University, University of San Francisco, and University of Wisconsin at Whitewater, and was the Writer-in-Residence at Holy Names University from 2012 to 2016.

His writing has appeared in several publications, including the Seattle Post-Intelligencer, San Francisco Chronicle, Houston Chronicle, San Antonio Express-News, Business Insider, and HuffPost. He was a contributor to the Ed Baxter Morning Show on iHeart Radio, and was also a frequent commentator on San Francisco's KGO Radio, as well as on several NPR shows.

Cipriani has received numerous awards for his disability advocacy work, including being named "Best Disability Advocate" by SF Weekly (2015), an "Agent of Change" by HuffPost (2015), and an "ABC7 Star" by KGO-TV (2016). He was also honored as the first blind Grand Marshal at San Francisco's 45th Annual Gay Pride Parade.

He currently works at the Center for Academic Excellence at Metropolitan State University in St. Paul, MN, where he helps students improve their writing skills.

Also Available

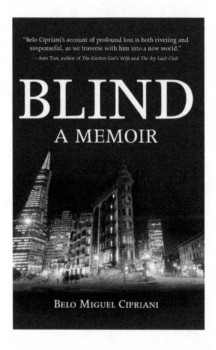

In the spring of 2007, Belo Cipriani was beaten and robbed of his sight at the hands of his childhood friends.

At the age of twenty-six, Belo found himself learning to walk, cook, and date in the dark. Armed with visual memory and his newly developed senses, Belo shows readers what the blind see. He narrates the recondite world of the blind, where microwaves, watches, and computers talk, and where guide dogs guard as well as lead.

"Belo Cipriani's account of profound loss is both riveting and suspenseful, as we traverse with him into a new world."
—Amy Tan, author of *The Joy Luck Club*

www.BeloCipriani.com